FIVE HOUSEKEEPING PRINCIPLES FOR THE Domestic Goddess

FIVE
HOUSEKEEPING PRINCIPLES FOR THE
Domestic Goddess

Find Joy Through Cleaning, Organising, and Unclogging Energy

Indiana Greene

Copyright © 2025 by Indiana Greene

All rights reserved. No part of this book may be reproduced or used in any manner without written permission of the copyright owner except for the use of quotations in a book review. For more information, contact: info@indianagreene.co.uk

First paperback edition 2025

978-1-80541-743-9 (Hardback)
978-1-80541-658-6 (paperback)
978-1-80541-573-2 (ebook)

www.indianagreene.co.uk

Table of Contents

About the Author vii

Introduction 1

Chapter 1: Cleaning with Water 17

Chapter 2: Unclogging Energy 47

Chapter 3: Chunk by Chunk (Step by Step) 77

Chapter 4: Zooming In 113

Chapter 5: Zooming Out 133

Chapter 6: Conclusion 159

About the Author

With a background spanning international corporate life and freelance consulting, I bring a unique perspective to the cleaning industry. My journey into this field was unexpected, having being diagnosed with bipolar and manic depression, making more than my fair share of mistakes and bad decision making, I found my vocation through cleaning. I now run a million-pound cleaning brand and businesses. And it came about through being just a cleaner. It literally saved my life. I was lucky enough to be influenced from my experience managing domestic arrangements for a vast range of clients varying from high-profile clients with very demanding standards. Cleaning for royalty through to hoarders.

These roles offered me invaluable insights into the psychology and logistics of providing top-tier services, as well as the challenges faced by both employers and employees in the domestic cleaning services sector. It was here that I witnessed first-hand the disconnect between expectations and realities, and the impact this had on both sides of the service equation.

After working for VVIP clients, I made what was a fairly unconventional decision to apply my hard-earned wisdom in an attempt to change what is an ugly duckling industry. Drawing from my experiences, I founded a cleaning company with a mission to bridge the gap between client expectations and service delivery, while prioritising the wellbeing and dignity of cleaning professionals. Cleaners are often considered as people who can't do anything else. The lowest end of the job market. But it occurred to me that it is actually one of the most fundamentally important roles that leads to fantastic mental health.

My view and approach are rooted in the belief that a well-maintained home is fundamental to a fulfilling life, and that achieving this requires a deep understanding of both client needs and industry realities. I've dedicated myself to creating a business model that fosters mutual respect, clear communication, and lasting relationships between clients and cleaners.

With years of experience and hundreds of employees under my belt, I've developed what I think is a unique philosophy that transforms house cleaning from a mundane chore into an essential component of a happy, healthy lifestyle.

Through this book, I share my insights and strategies to help you navigate the complexities of managing a home, finding the right support, together with the aim of enhancing your quality of life.

Whether you are a cleaning professional or a homemaker, my goal is to empower you with the knowledge and understanding to create a home environment that truly reflects your vision for living or working.

Introduction

Be it official or unofficial many of us have the responsibility of looking after our home. Many housewives and househusbands find housekeeping overwhelming and it's the worst part of their life, the bit they dread doing. So much so that they keep putting off tasks, seeing cleaning and looking after the home as a chore and something they regret as being part of their life. They only do it if they absolutely have to and things get so bad it can no longer be ignored. Ironically I found it takes more energy to ignore doing something than doing the job itself.

Even if you see yourself lucky enough to outsource your cleaning, it still can be strenuous relying on someone else. Does your housekeeper focus on areas important to you? Do they understand what areas need disinfecting? Are they able to tidy as they go? Do they care or cut corners? Are they trustworthy?

Conversely many of the housekeepers who work for me have aired concerns such as:

- My client just critiques my work with no guidance on their personal needs.
- They won't share with me their priorities or preferences regarding cleaning products and presentation.
- I just get complained at for everything I do. I feel my client looks down on me like I am a lesser person.
- It seems my client resents paying for the services. They have no problem buying endless expensive cleaning products but resent having to pay for my efforts.

Whether you are a cleaner, housekeeper, housewife or househusband there seems to be deep-rooted prejudices that cleaning is a job for a "lesser person".

The idea that cleaning is a "lesser" occupation is rooted in a combination of historical, cultural and societal biases, which have evolved over time. These prejudices stem from several sources.

1. Historical Class Divisions

- In many societies, cleaning and domestic labour have historically been assigned to lower social classes or enslaved individuals. In feudal systems, for example, the elite delegated physical labour to peasants or servants reinforcing the notion that cleaning was "beneath" the wealthy and educated.
- During the Industrial Revolution, domestic service became a common occupation for working-class women and immigrants, further associating cleaning with low economic and social status.

2. Gender Roles and Patriarchy

- Traditionally, cleaning and household management have been assigned to women as part of their "natural" role in the home. These tasks were seen as an extension of caregiving, which, though essential, were undervalued because they

occurred in the private sphere rather than in the public, economically productive world.
- Men who took on cleaning roles often faced stigma for performing what was perceived as "women's work", reinforcing the idea that such work was demeaning.

3. Colonialism and Racism

- In many colonial contexts, domestic work was relegated to indigenous populations or enslaved individuals, creating an intersection between race, labour and power. This entrenched the belief that cleaning was for those considered "inferior," and these associations persist in some societies.

4. Economic Structures and Capitalism

- Under capitalism, jobs that are perceived as low-skill or manual labor often pay less and receive less respect. Cleaning, though essential, is considered "unskilled", even though it requires significant effort, attention to detail and expertise.
- The invisibility of cleaning work—often performed behind the scenes—contributes to its undervaluation.

5. Cultural Narratives and Media

- Popular culture has often depicted cleaners or housekeepers as background characters, or individuals with little ambition. These portrayals reinforce stereotypes and diminish the perceived importance of their work.

6. Modern-Day Prejudices

- Today, cleaning is often outsourced to people from marginalised communities, immigrants or those from lower socioeconomic backgrounds. This reinforces a hierarchy in which cleaning is associated with inequality and perceived as undesirable work.

Challenging These Beliefs

To combat these prejudices, it's important to:

- Acknowledge the value of cleaning: It is indispensable to personal health, public hygiene and overall societal functioning.
- Pay and treat workers fairly: Providing fair wages and dignified working conditions elevates the perception of the work itself.
- Challenge stereotypes: Highlight stories of skilled, professional cleaners and emphasise the expertise involved in the field.

- Shift cultural narratives: Encourage media and educational systems to portray cleaning work with respect and appreciation.

These deeply rooted beliefs about cleaning as "lesser" are a reflection of broader social inequities and require a collective effort to dismantle.

Many of us feel unappreciated for what we do in the home and possibly see it as a demotion in life. The person who looks after the home is possibly perceived as less important than an earner or provider. Or are we feeling constantly unfairly compared to Marie Kondo or Nigella Lawson? Maybe we even feel resentful that the task seems to fall on us alone. Maybe you want to get to a place where you feel passionate about your home and want to keep making it even better. You might even have a family and want to give them the very best life and understand the importance of a good home life, but just need a few more effective ways of doing this.

Whatever the reason, if you would like to release even more of your inner "domestic goddess" and get more meaning out of looking after your home and making a space to flourish, recuperate and love, then this book is for you.

I asked my friends and family what they thought the definition of a "domestic goddess" was. Here are some answers:

- a being full of light
- a woman who knows and loves herself
- someone who makes domestic chores into an in-the-moment happy spiritual practice
- someone who loves her home (both her physical home and spiritual home)
- a woman who is a magician and alchemist with everything she touches
- someone who really knows about genuine gratitude (towards herself and others)
- a creative being who sings from within
- a person of any gender who comes from her heart.

Cleaning has become my chosen vocation in life, and in this book, I aim to convince you that, metaphorically, you may share the same calling. Cleaning your inner and outer world is an essential part of becoming that domestic goddess and getting true value out of this part of your life.

A considerable amount of money was spent on my education as a child, and investments were made into developing my know-how as a businessperson. My father built a business based on inner growth which taught me how to have inner discipline.

Then many years later, deep down, after much searching, pain, dreadful mistakes and growth I realised I was only meant to be a cleaner—nothing more, nothing less. In retrospect I realise most of my work involved cleaning in one form or another. Be it as a communications ttrainer and change manager and coach.

I have now been a professional cleaner for over twenty years, and I have founded and grown a company where I employ other full-time cleaners to help our clients transform their living environments and in turn help them live happier lives. It has been the most challenging task I have ever undertaken, as the company has hundreds of moving parts.

However, at the heart of the business lies the challenge of dealing with human beings, and at the core of every human being is the desire to improve things.

I don't think it's pretentious to say that this desire to improve is something we all have in common. Helping people have a home that supports their lives has become a privilege to undertake.

As I share my experiences with you, hopefully this book will inspire you to explore the qualitative elements of how to approach unclogging, organising and cleaning—whether you clean your own home or prefer to outsource to a professional cleaning business or individual.

It was clear to me many people viewed my new career as a demotion, but I hope to impart to you how, through making multitudes of mistakes, much repetition and practise, I started to find cleaning liberating. I am now truly proud to be called simply a "cleaner".

Being able to transform spaces and demonstrate love and care by making spaces beautiful for my clients made me proud as well as allowed me to be present for my sons as they grew up. How many of us yearn to have such a job where we don't feel pulled in all directions?

After time I became a highly sought-after housekeeper for palaces, houses, caravans and hoarders alike. No challenge scared me, and I started to formulate my five cleaning principles, which I discovered maybe applicable to all of us.

The aim of this book is to explore both the philosophical and practical elements of transforming and looking after a home. Be it your own home or if you choose to make cleaning your vocation. Most cleaning books concentrate on practical cleaning hacks which are fabulous and fun. This book, however, has a different emphasis and looks at the spiritual aspects behind using the tips and hacks.

Many people leave the cleaning profession feeling undervalued or appreciated. I find this to be a sad reality. I believe it's one of the most important jobs in the world. What would happen if we stopped cleaning, collectively or as individuals? I hope these cleaning principles help to create meaning in such an important role.

In order to have a beautiful home you have to love and cherish yourself first. My staff are amazing and I believe we should treat our cleaners like customers and in turn they can help you transform your home through giving love. It always shocks me when I think how badly some cleaners get treated.

Being a domestic goddess does not naturally come to all of us, especially nowadays. In the modern world we are expected to bring up children, juggle uniforms, washing, cleaning, ironing, healthy eating, clean up after daily chaos, homework, recycling, shopping and much more. For many this is on top of a full-time job. Being a domestic goddess does take time and time has to be allocated to making the home run smoothly. In this book I hope to show you the five spiritual and practical tips to run your home efficiently and with clarity of purpose. So rather than housekeeping being a chore it becomes an essential step-by-step act of facilitating happiness and growth. In fact something that becomes an important and rewarding part of your life.

It's a bit like pursuing physical health through running, weight training, spin classes, etc. To gain the rewards you have to be consistent. If you don't do it step by step, day by day we have to face the consequences of not looking after ourselves in this way. It can be a source of immense unhappiness. But when you get into the habit of following the principles outlined in this book, you'll actually start enjoying it and the benefits it brings to you. Just like exercise.

It inspires you to eat healthier, which in turn helps you feel better. You feel excited that you can fit into your favourite clothes and the benefits go on, seeping into all aspects of your life. This book is about helping you define what you need to do to look after a happy home. If you live alone or with a partner or friends/family. What do you feel your relationship is with housekeeping?

On a slightly different note, during my time running a cleaning business I have come across many clients where there is a deep-rooted sense of resentment in having to pay for a cleaner. They may feel that cleaning is an unwelcome problem in their life and are entitled and that somehow their mess should miraculously disappear. I have come across many clients whose attitude is if the cleaner misses one thing, such as a cobweb, they are entitled to a free clean. Even if the cleaner had bust a gut for five hours they think they should not pay. Cleaning is always a work in progress and things will always need doing. This book helps you on this journey. It's about progress not perfection.

By understanding these principles, we can engage with the spiritual and practical aspects of cleaning and enjoy a more beautiful and happy home and appreciate its true value.

I believe good housekeeping comes with focus, practice and a strategic approach, which is what I want to share with you.

To the far left of the spectrum, some choose to ignore cleaning altogether, believing that ignoring cleanliness will create its own ecosystem, similar to those who neglect dental hygiene or hair washing. My mother created beautiful spaces, but cleaning was not a priority for her, so I partly understand this perspective.

On the far-right end of the spectrum, some people with obsessive compulsive disorder feel highly anxious if cleaning is not done very regularly, and everything must have its exact place at the right time and any deviation from this is seen as a catastrophe. Wherever we are on the spectrum, we all need a solution to the need to live well in an environment that supports who we are. Our house starts to represent who you are and becomes a reflection of your inner state of mind.

Background

This book is about the fundamentals behind the skills and *approach* to cleaning and not so much the day-to-day tips on *what* to clean. Those things are important and I share many practical tips through other resources, but this book is more about the spiritual and practical aspects of housekeeping that underpin the fundamentals of keeping a healthy and luxurious home.

I believe that with some self-love and care and a little focus on these five principles, everyone can have luxury. Whether you live in a palace, stately home, house, apartment or caravan. Whatever shape or size, your home is your space, your sanctuary.

Before we go into this, I want to touch on the art of cleaning so that we can create a nice atmosphere to spend time with people we love (if being social is integral to your happiness) or even create a space for you to cherish yourself, show yourself love and respect, or both.

I believe a home should be a place we can feel safe. Similar to the feelings we try to impart to a cherished newborn child—our first aim being to make them feel safe and secure.

You are their home, their world in their infancy. I believe whatever age we are we all need a space to call home so we not only survive and feel safe, but we also need a place to love that supports us with a sense of belonging and self-belief. Home should be a place where we are shielded from the world and where we can let our guard down. How do we turn our house into a home, rather than just a place to eat and sleep? A house? Four walls and a roof? It can be a place to find comfort and connection and a place to flourish.

I discovered these principles as a result of cleaning everything from palaces to caravans, from people who have OCD to hoarders, over a timespan of twenty years, day in and day out. I was driven to master housekeeping and these principles can help you do that far quicker than it took me.

Our aim should be to create spaces that actually have an impact on our wellbeing. I'll show you how housekeeping can lead to happiness, a sense of inner growth.

Have you ever experienced how a room changed your mood, or walked into a space and wanted to stay there? Maybe it was the warmth and flickering sound of a fire, the sunshine rays gleaming warmth through the windows or it just reminded you of home?

We may not have control over events affecting us in much of this world but we have control over homemaking, which in turn can inspire us to be better human beings, to create the best possible environment for our health and wellbeing. We have the power to shape our environment, which in turn can inspire us to make the world a better place.

The Backbone: The Five Cleaning Principles

I believe life is a training ground. I have to admit I am quite uneducated having been to many schools in my early life due to my bohemian mother. So writing a book surprises me and the thought was quite daunting. But my early years taught me that change is inevitable and equipped me with a certain degree of courage to explore new things and places. Even my cleaning company is based on personal growth and development. I feel there is always something to learn.

Like a Buddhist monk, I believe we remove the dirt to liberate ourselves from darkness. We clean to bring literal lightness into our home. The act of cleansing our home is to free ourselves from unhealthy attachments, physically and spiritually. To take time to cleanse your home is extremely fulfilling.

I liken it to learning geography at school. Until you actually visit a country you can't get a full sense of the culture. It's the same as homemaking—until you commit to love it and explore every part of your home, you can't make it yours. It's part of the magical process of homemaking.

There are mountains of very helpful video blogs out there on saving time when cleaning but it's important in this day and age in our fast-paced life to forget that actually the journey does matter and the actual act of cleaning helps cleanse the mind.

You don't need to have access to top home designers to have a wonderful home.

I know friends who have only bought from charity shops and only purchased up-cycled furniture. You just need to know what makes you happy, brings you positive energy. By trusting your instinct on what you find pleasing will allow you to develop your very own unique signature style that represent your unique qualities and values.

We all want to be efficient and find the quickest way to do things in our busy lives but actually the process of cleaning has an innate value in itself. Easy to forget in our fast-paced modern world.

Children are growing up without a clue about what cleaning is and the true value it brings to our lives. I hope in this book to inspire a little, to create meaning once again in the fundamental art and process of cleaning. I would love nothing more than to reintroduce cleaning into the school curriculum. It would help so much in this day and age of mental health issues being at its highest ever.

I believe if we live life in a careless way our mind will be cluttered but if we try living our live contentiously, almost deliberately, life will become pure again. If your heart is pure, in turn the world looks positive and even brighter. I have found this in turn helps me to be kinder to others and in turn it helps me feel more at peace. Through the act of cleaning you also cultivate your mind.

Cleaning is not considered a cumbersome or lowly task in Japan and I found myself, after a very troubled life, through cleaning, finding lightness and happiness.

I learnt the five cleaning principles through literally thousands of cleaning hours and then through observing the best cleaners in action. Like Buddhist monks and the top professionals in this field, you too can find enlightenment through following my steps.

CHAPTER ONE

Cleaning with Water

Water is the vital humour of the arid earth, flowing with unceasing vigour through the branching veins, replenishing all parts.

LEONARDO DA VINCI

I started my cleaning journey many years ago and it took me a while to realise the powerful part water could play in my housekeeping journey.

Before I go into cleaning with water I want to cover some of the basics and why we use cleaning products and establish when they are and are not necessary.

Cleaning Products

Before we look at cleaning with water in what I call cleansing cleaning, I would like to explore "cleaning products" a little.

There is an overwhelming variety of cleaning products out there. Just look at the rows of shelves in supermarkets dedicated to home cleaning. Perhaps through intensive marketing we have created the illusion that each surface needs its own specialised product and that we possibly have an unhealthy addiction to chemicals.

Through looking at a few basics and understanding them we can reduce the number of products we think we need in the home and in turn save money and avoid frustration.

In my cleaning business we use three basic products watered down in three separate spray bottles:

1. diluted washing up liquid for glass, mirrors and most surfaces including floors
2. vinegar or diluted limescale remover to remove hard water stains and build-up
3. watered down disinfectant for targeted cleaning

That's it! You may want to buy specialised cleaning products for things such as wood, silver, brass, etc. but that is what I call specialised cleaning and that does not form part of our more regular daily and weekly tasks.

Let's look at cleaning product fundamentals and what we use them for.

- **Anti-Germ Products:** For disinfecting high-touch areas. Use these selectively and only where needed for targeted cleaning.
- **Acidic Cleaners (e.g. vinegar):** Ideal for dissolving limescale and works well on hard water stains in the bathroom and kitchen but isn't suitable for all surfaces, such as granite or marble.
- **Alkaline Cleaners (e.g. dish soap):** Alkaline cleaners are best for breaking down grease and grime. Dish soap is versatile, affordable and mild enough for many surfaces. It's often all you need for general cleaning.

Watch Out for Overly Complex Products

Many products claim to be multi-surface or have added shine, but they sometimes leave a stubborn film that's harder to remove than the dirt itself—especially on glass surfaces, where residue can create streaks.

There is a common misconception that we need to use chemicals in our entire home to keep it germ-free.

Let's split cleaning into two types:

1. "Aesthetic" cleaning: Keeping spaces looking fresh, tidy and dust free.
2. Targeted cleaning: Germ removal, but not all surfaces require sanitisation.

To know which type of cleaning we should do we need to understand the journey of germs.

Germs get into our home on our hands, shoes, bags or objects like groceries. Once they're inside, they settle on surfaces where we spread them such as on doorknobs, countertops, light switches and bathroom areas.

These are the spots where targeted cleaning should be highly effective to reduce germs that may pose health risks.

The good news is this is typically needed for less than one percent of the house surfaces so it's totally achievable. I get frustrated when people say harmful germs breed around the house for no reason. Germs only come into the home when we bring them in ourselves.

Two Effective Methods to Remove Germs

1. Using Approved Cleaning Products (labelled to say they kill "99.9%" of bacteria and viruses)

However, beware. To work effectively, they often need to sit on the surface for five minutes or as indicated on the label. This "dwell time" allows the active ingredients to break down the germs. Regularly switching cleaning cloths is also helpful to avoid cross-contamination.

2. Rinsing with Running Water

Like a surgeon's handwashing method, holding items under running water from the tap removes germs and washes them down the drain.

This is particularly effective for items like cutting boards, after using raw meat, utensils, and produce that can tolerate water and a dash of washing liquid or vinegar—you don't necessarily need chemical disinfectants. For best results, scrub with a brush or sponge under the water. Use cleaning products for high-touch areas that can't be rinsed under a sink like a door handle for example.

Together, these methods help maintain a safe, germ-conscious home without excessive chemical use.

There are thousands of microbes in our home—most of which are not harmful.

Rather than trying to sanitise germs through the entire home—which would be time-consuming, expensive and unnecessary—it's more practical to focus on high-touch zones, especially after returning from public spaces.

Benefits of Targeted Cleaning

It not only saves effort and time but also avoids overuse of harsh chemicals, which can irritate skin, harm indoor air quality, and potentially, over time contribute to antimicrobial resistance.

By focusing on high-contact areas only, we can strike a healthy balance between maintaining a clean and safe environment and not overdoing it.

It's best to find a product that actually says "kills 99.9% of viruses and bacteria" so we can be sure it's been tested.

Too Much Product

Is there such thing as using too much cleaning product? By doing so it can create more problems than it solves. I watch all these wonderful videos on social media that look great with tons of bubbles and copious amounts of products. It looks great but believe me most of us just don't have the time to spend rinsing the bubbles from the overuse of products.

Firstly, the problem it can create is "residue build-up".

Less is more. When excess product is left on surfaces, it often dries into a film that attracts more dirt and dust. This residue can actually make spaces look and feel less clean, as it traps grime and makes surfaces sticky. The film can also harbour bacteria, ironically reducing the hygiene level of the very surfaces you're trying to sanitise. Instead of wiping bacteria away, the product film can trap and even create a breeding ground for it.

Secondly, it can make cleaning work harder.

Overusing products requires extra rinsing and wiping to remove the excess, which means more scrubbing and water use. This makes cleaning more labour-intensive and time-consuming. Just like with shower gel on your body, you only need enough product to help remove grime effectively. More doesn't equate to better; it simply means more effort is required to rinse it off.

Thirdly, you need to know how to use just the right amount.

Dilute the product when possible. Some products can be diluted with water without sacrificing effectiveness, especially for light cleaning jobs. For spray cleaners, a light mist is usually enough. A small amount spread evenly across the surface works better than soaking it. Follow the manufacturer instructions. Product labels often give clear instructions on the right amount to use. By following them, you can avoid waste and ensure the product performs as intended.

By using just the necessary amount, you not only make cleaning easier but also reduce waste, cut costs and ensure surfaces stay truly clean and hygienic.

Now back to cleansing with water and why. Up until the age of fifteen years old I lived a very bohemian lifestyle. Everything was very relaxed, no rules at all. I can honestly say I can't remember having fixed mealtimes; we could help ourselves from the larder whenever we wanted. I dread to think what I smelt like. There was no system for washing clothes! I think I must have moved house over thirty times by the time I was fifteen and went to over twenty different schools. We had no cleaning products in the house as far as I recall. We did have washing up liquid though. Funnily enough, now I am in my fifties I have come full circle and rarely use anything stronger than washing up liquid. My mother taught me the importance of drinking water.

When I left my mother to live with my father at fifteen to embark on a programme of work experience in his business based on personal growth, it became clear I was never going to pass my exams. The schools I had been to and the constant school changing meant I had not had the consistency in education to make it through them.

I went from a free living environment to where everything became strictly monitored and required immense discipline. For the first time I had deadlines. I had to be on time to start work, breaks, lunch. I started by sticking labels on envelopes and I had to do that day in and day out for many months as part of my induction. I attended communication training where everything from my tone, pitch and speed of voice was analysed as well as my physical impact. I became part of my Fathers business, the called 'Programmes Ltd'. It was I believe the first telephone marketing business so we had to master communication skills.

We had cleaners at home and the smell of bleach, wood polish, etc. made me feel I was living in a luxurious environment. I stopped drinking water believing that tea or coffee was a better substitute. I put on so much weight. I believe, in retrospect, as I was eating different foods and no longer any pure water. My weight became a big source of unhappiness and pain.

Now to have a weight I am happy with, drinking water is crucial to my health. A clear sign of not drinking enough water is when our urine is yellow or potent. Or headaches and depression. I now have a drinking water alarm on my phone. It is thought that women should drink 2.7 litres of water a day, men 3.7 litres. How much do you drink? Being hydrated is an essential part of life and most certainly needed when cleaning your home.

I like to fill up a glass tank of filtered water with a tap on it. I put sliced lemons/limes/oranges into the tank and keep topping up my glass throughout the day. It's fun to add ice in hot weather. In my cleaning business I come across so many staff who do not hydrate properly throughout the day. Their excuse is they don't want to have to keep going to the loo. I try to encourage then that their health is more important. You are literally slowly poisoning yourself if you don't drink enough. To be a domestic goddess, water is key for your own inner body as well as your outer life, your home. Let's now look at cleaning a home with water.

We may have addictions to cleaning products believing that in order to be safe and hygienic in our homes we must use chemicals. I discovered this to be totally untrue. Is this how you feel? Maybe you know someone with these views?

Here I share why and how cleaning with water actually does work and that typically it can be effectively used on at least seventy percent of your home.

I am not against cleaning products but I advise to find natural ones that will bring nice scents and enhance your cleaning, not mask bad cleaning habits. Nancy Birtwhistle's book *Clean and Green: 101 Hint and Tips for a More Eco-friendly Home* is my favourite book with incredibly doable tips on green cleaning.

The number of times when going to a new home my clients complained that all their previous cleaner used to do was flick a fluffy duster around and spray air freshener around the house.

This chapter explains proper cleaning practices to ensure your home is truly clean.

Cleaning Motives

First of all, let's explore our real motives as to why we clean:

- To make the house look good?
- To make the house smell good?
- To remove germs?
- I don't know
- I've been told I should do it
- I find it therapeutic
- Something else?

Chemical Vs Water Housekeeping

The problem, I believe, lies in the lack of knowledge about proper foundational cleaning techniques.

We typically spray a cleaning product, rub it in and call it a day. However, this method doesn't effectively remove all dirt like we think.

Instead, a portion still remains on the surface, mixed with chemicals from the cleaning products and then ingrained into the material. If you use soap or shower gel on your body and do not rinse with water the product soaks too much into your body.

While this might not appear to be a significant problem initially, repeated use exacerbates the build-up of dirty chemical residue.

This is not a great way for keeping our spaces truly clean. We're bombarded by persuasive advertising from brands in supermarkets, leading us to believe—sometimes erroneously—that their products are essential and the only way to eradicate germs.

It's surprising how many of my clients actually admit they don't know how to clean. Clients even pay me to tidy up after their children as well as clean.

Their lives are chaotic, and their home just leads to more stress in a world that is already so high paced, so many of us never get to take a breath. Where is their sanctuary?

It seems there is a generation where we have lost the art of housekeeping. I clearly remember asking my grandmother on my father's side why her home was so perfect. Why did I feel so safe and happy? She explained that in her day, at school they did domestic science (home economics) which included: laundry (washing/ironing/folding), cleaning, cooking and sewing.

In fact, both my grandmothers knew how to run a perfect home. They were always pristine and the most comforting environments to be in. I went to my grandmothers to feel safe, secure and happy.

On reflection I realise partly why this was the case. Everything was pristine and every item was either useful or beautiful. Everything in their homes had a purpose. There were no areas that made me feel stressed or clogged my energy. I could just be me at peace with no stress.

I feel many of us have never been around a mother or grandmother who has shown us how to look after our home in this high-paced world. It seems many of us have lost the art of domestic science.

While running my business I have always been curious as to why, when employing Spanish, Portuguese, Bulgarian and Polish women, they already have fabulous cleaning skills.

When I ask why they feel cleaning comes so natural to them, the majority say that they learnt from their mothers and grandmothers from a very young age through watching and helping.

I would love to know the number of British children who learn to clean from their elders against the number in the Mediterranean. I suspect less.

On arrival at many clients' homes children spend so much time on their iPads and most don't even know how to wash up or take used crockery to the sink after dinner. Of course this is not always the case, but I suspect possibly less so than a few generations ago.

Seventy Percent Water

Let's put H_2O into context. About seventy percent of our bodies are made up of water. As a rule of thumb, we can only last around three days without water. It's vital to our health and an essential part of personal wellbeing and life. I constantly recall my mother's constant reminder, "Drink more water!"—a piece of advice that couldn't be more accurate.

Consider this. Approximately seventy percent of the Earth's surface is covered by water. Yet, we fear that water is not powerful enough to use as the main cleaning tool. Without water our world could not survive.

Now, let me explain. We need to use water in at least seventy percent of our home surfaces. Before we proceed, let's explore these revelations.

The Components of Water

Water is a remarkable solvent for cleaning due to its inherent polarity. The water molecule consists of two hydrogen atoms and one oxygen atom, with the oxygen atom possessing a slight negative charge while the hydrogen atoms carry a slight positive charge.

This uneven distribution of charge creates a polar molecule, enabling water to form hydrogen bonds with other polar or charged substances.

This unique property allows water to dissolve a wide range of compounds, making it an effective solvent for cleaning various surfaces. Water's ability to dissolve substances like dirt, grease and grime is particularly advantageous, as it can surround and disperse these particles effectively.

The ability of water to interact with a multitude of substances makes it an essential component in most cleaning processes, contributing to its universal role in maintaining cleanliness and hygiene.

Here's an interesting question: when cleaning your own home, what percentage of the surfaces do you clean using cleaning products, and what percentage do you clean with just water? And if you do use a cleaning product, what percentage of the surfaces do you rinse off with water afterwards?

Consider This Analogy

When we shower or bathe, most of us reach for shower gel, bubble bath or soap to cleanse out bodies. But what's next after using our favourite product?

We rinse with water. If you had to make a choice to use either water *or* the product for the rest of your life, which one would you use? Most of us would instinctively choose water. Why? This is my point. Because water is the true essence of cleanliness.

Surgical hand antisepsis requires clean water to rinse the hands after applying the medicated soap.

Relying solely on cleaning products, akin to using shower gels without rinsing them off, would leave behind a residue that clogs our skin, preventing it from breathing naturally.

In my opinion, the majority of commercial cleaning products are a con and actually make cleaning more difficult. Of course, there are some fabulous natural products out there, but don't be swayed solely by attractive packaging or the label "natural" on cleaning products.

On my extensive journey in the realm of cleaning, spanning over twenty years and accumulating more than 37,440 cleaning hours,

I've encountered a diverse array of people from various walks of life, from royalty, professionals, homemakers, hoarders, infirm and even professional housekeepers who are disgusted by the thought of only using water and are addicted to the use of cleaning products, believing that if their house doesn't smell of Pledge and bleach, it's not truly clean. How addicted are you to cleaning products?

Over the years, I've observed a spectrum of attitudes towards cleaning products, ranging from addiction to aversion. However, I've come to realise that a healthy balance is essential in your home. A healthy number of bacteria and viruses are healthy and good.

Apparently after our Covid lockdowns there was a massive surge in illnesses as we came out into the world again. We had lost some of our resistance to these germs. So generally, a more balanced approach to cleaning is good in my opinion rather than spreading everything with bleach!

Understanding the Importance of Water

My mother was a truly beautiful woman inside and out, and sadly no longer with us. Many would describe her as a "hippy" or someone who embraced alternative living long before it became mainstream.

She was ahead of her time when it came to organic living practices. In my younger years, I didn't even know that washing hands was a thing. Our house, as far as I can recall, was rarely cleaned, if ever. I can't even remember us having a hoover, though we did have a broom—I'm not sure if it was ever used.

At best the sinks would only receive a brief swish of water with our fingers. Over time, a home develops its own ecosystem and you build your own immunity. As a young child I was fascinated how Rastafarians may choose to not wash their hair and let their hair take its natural course using only water. Now I've discovered they use baking soda, apple cider vinegar or aloe vera.

As explained in my teenage years during the 1980s, I transitioned from living in various homes in the countryside, immersed in a bohemian environment, to moving to the bustling city of London with my father.

To my amazement, my father employed housekeepers. I was utterly fascinated by their presence and the immaculate state of our home. The sight of vacuum marks on the carpets and the lingering scent of alien potent cleaning products. It was my first encounter with what I perceived as luxury and comfort. Gradually, I began to associate these elements with a sense of opulence.

After experiencing many adventures in life, I found myself in my thirties as a single mother to two incredible lively vivacious young sons. Determined to find a vocation that would allow me to balance work with being there for the school runs, homework and evening meals, I made the bold decision to become a cleaner. I had no experience whatsoever.

Despite not having a clue on how to clean as a professional, I was driven by a deep desire to find a fulfilling career that aligned with my responsibilities as a parent. Contrary to the prevailing stigma surrounding the profession, I believed it held the potential for job satisfaction and pride.

So, I embarked on my cleaning journey armed with determination but lacking experience. Through trial and error—admittedly, with a lot more error than I care to admit—I learnt the ropes of the trade.

I destroyed hoovers by incorrectly fitting the bag, damaged oven tops by using the wrong products and left stubborn stains that were impossible to remove.

I learnt the hard way about using the wrong scourer, which resulted in damage to chrome taps and mirrors, spraying harsh limescale removers on bathroom grout and dying it blue, damaging kitchen fronts by spraying strong products and leaving spray marks. The list of my mishaps and missteps goes on and on.

Additionally, I relied heavily on bleach and strong cleaning products, coupled with an excessive use of kitchen roll instead of cloths to wipe off the excess.

Within just three months, I developed severe asthma which I can only link to the use of harsh chemicals. My doctor explained to me that you can develop hypersensitivity and can trigger the development of the triad (asthma, hay fever and eczema). Not only was this detrimental to my health, but it was also financially unsustainable—I found myself spending more money on kitchen roll and cleaning products than I was earning.

So, this book shows my full circle journey, embracing a more sustainable and holistic approach to cleaning and understanding through cleaning day in day out for over twenty years, the value of water as my greatest companion.

Through using water to clean as my main ingredient, my health improved and my cleaning results improved ten-fold and became enjoyable and effortless.

I carried out a survey a few years ago where we cleaned two properties mainly with water and two properties with cleaning products. The properties cleaned with water were scored higher in terms of perceived cleanliness without the participants knowing why.

In my housekeeping business, I prioritise training all my staff to clean using water properly first. Once this fundamental skill is mastered, I permit the use of cleaning products, but with a crucial caveat: they must be as natural as possible and serve to enhance the cleaning process rather than merely mask inadequate practices. It's a great discipline to teach—sometimes seeing is believing.

Introduction to the Wet, Dry, Buff Technique

We're all familiar with the never-ending cycle of cleaning, just as soon as it's cleaned another week has arrived and it's time to do it again. Maintaining a spotless home at all times is not always feasible.

However, shifting our focus from solely the end result to the process itself by focusing on the process of cleaning and assessing your space, we find satisfaction in the incremental improvements we make. This is where my chunk-by-chunk approach (detailed later in this book) becomes invaluable.

I advise alternating between rooms that are not used as frequently and concentrating regularly on high-traffic areas by categorising areas as high, medium or low traffic. In the upcoming chapters, we'll delve into creating daily, weekly and monthly cleaning schedules for your home, akin to caring for yourself—prioritising high-traffic areas like teeth, hands and hair, while allocating less attention to low-traffic.

Now, onto my best-kept secret: the science behind cleaning with water. I'll unravel the wet, dry, buff technique and introduce you to our best friend in cleaning—the microfibre cloth.

These cloths have the capacity to hold ninety-eight times their weight in liquid volume and create an inhospitable environment for bacteria to remain. The correct tools are essential. For instance, we typically use around seventy of these cloths in a single home (that's a full top-to-bottom clean). Yes, that magic number again.

For the wet, dry, buff technique, use a wet cloth for the initial wipe, regularly rinsed with water, a separate one for drying and a final for buffing things, such as mirrors, glass, taps and shower heads. It's essential to change the wet cloth at least once for each separate room and regularly rinse it during use.

The dry cloth plays a pivotal role in lifting dirt. This is the part that lifts the germs into the cloth. After the dry application, and once the dry cloth becomes damp, it's done is job and can't lift any more germs. Using this method correctly you can remove ninety-nine percent of viruses and ninety-three percent of bacteria. Get to know your cloths and how they work like a painter with their brush. It's part of the true art of cleaning.

My experiences working with hotels left me horrified by the realisation that hotels and airplanes are notorious breeding grounds for germs because they don't follow this procedure. It's alarming to discover that some resorts and airlines utilise used guest towels to buff surfaces cleaned with chemical products, potentially spreading harmful bacteria and bodily fluids. Many of the germs that live on dry surfaces can live for a very long time— days or in some cases even weeks. Therefore, to combat this, I carry a dirty cloth bag with me from one room to another. As soon as our dry cloth becomes damp, it's done its job and it is promptly replaced and sealed in a biodegradable plastic bag to prevent cross-contamination. Our dry cloth should be replaced approximately every five to ten minutes. I prefer to use biodegradable plastic bags for the environment's sake.

The buff technique is primarily for use on chrome, mirrors and glass windows (bathrooms and taps in general) to remove any small smears and residue. It will provide the perfect finishing touch.

To summarise, this technique, while primarily about cleanliness, can also be applied to aesthetics. We don't want to spend time cleaning a window only to leave streaky marks and damp windowsills, as this could potentially cause all sorts of problems. Instead, by using the wet, dry, buff method, we are not only ensuring hygiene and cleanliness, but we are also enhancing aesthetics and shine. This is cleaning to give the wow factor.

Partner in Grime: The Microfibre Cloth

I love that analogy! Comparing cleaning with a microfibre cloth to an artist's brushstroke brings an element of artistry and mindfulness to a task that is often seen as routine. Trusting the process, like knowing when a painting is complete, is such a wise approach. Overdoing it can not only be counterproductive but can also take away from the satisfaction of the act itself.

It's about being present and confident in each swipe, knowing when enough is enough. In a way, it's a form of letting go—trusting that you've done what's necessary without the need for perfectionism. How did this philosophy change my relationship with everyday tasks? I certainly learnt to trust myself further.

The Foundations of a Microfibre Cloth

A dry microfibre cloth's ability to lift bacteria is based on the intricate structure of the microfibre material itself. Let's delve into detail.

Microfibre is a synthetic material composed of extremely fine fibres, usually less than one denier in diameter. These fibres are split into even finer sub-fibres, creating a large surface area and tiny spaces between fibres that can trap and hold particles, including bacteria and viruses.

When a dry microfibre cloth is used to wipe a surface, the fibres of the cloth work to physically remove particles from the surface through a process known as "mechanical action". The fibres can reach into small crevices and lift particles out by trapping them in the spaces between fibres.

Additionally, the fibres of microfibre cloth have a very high surface area to volume ratio, which means there is a lot of surface area available to pick up and hold particles. This property is further enhanced by the ability of the fibres to generate static electricity, which can attract and hold particles such as bacteria.

I am in a mission to find a cloth that achieves these results without being made of plastic. I justify its use currently as they are reusable. I have cloths that have lasted me years.

Cloth Confidence

When learning to use the cloth, it's all about getting cloth confidence. For general cleaning, one or two damp swipes with the cloth and it's done.

When learning to use the cloths I have noticed many go over the same area again and again. This is not necessary due to the nature of the cloth. This is why you can clean like a professional with speed with very little practice.

The combination of mechanical action and the large surface area of microfibre fibres makes it an effective tool to remove germs from surfaces. However, it's important to note that while the cloth does remove grime from a surface, it does not kill them. Therefore, to re-use the cloths they must be laundered between uses to remove the germs, therefore it is crucial to keep them bagged up until the wash.

Cloth Care

1. Wash the microfibre cloths at a minimum of sixty degrees to ensure the eradication of germs captured in the fabric of your cloths.
2. Do not use softener in the wash, as it causes the cloths to lose their ability to absorb water.
3. Line dry your cloths so they retain their porous nature and do not become static.

The Process of Cleansing

The anatomy of cleaning a home typically includes various tasks from dusting and vacuuming (not just floors but walls as well with the right attachments) to mopping and disinfecting surfaces.

However, it's essential to distinguish between the right and wrong approaches to these tasks. Personally, I'm a staunch advocate for the simplicity and effectiveness of plain water as a go-to solution for most cleaning surfaces.

Paired with the incredible microfibre cloth, water can achieve far more than one might imagine, despite the pervasive marketing of chemical products. Water: the miracle cleaner that can make all your dirty problems disappear, or so they say.

Cleaning Product Hoarding

I can tell a lot about a person by what's under the kitchen sink that typically stores cleaning products. I mostly find lots and lots of products for all sorts of things. Many have not been used for years. Be careful when out shopping. Do you really need another different smelling kitchen cleaner? It amazes me how so many of us buy cleaning products that in all truth will never be used. It satisfies our feeling that "yes, I will clean that kitchen" but then find other things more important to do. A commitment to using the wet, dry, buff technique with a microfibre cloth might be a better solution to buying yet another cleaning product that may never gets used.

What Can Water Handle and Rebel Against?

Now, let's discuss the materials that water can handle like a professional: metal, glass, ceramics, plastic, some wood and fabric. These materials are quite like the "A-grade children" of the cleaning world. They're easy to clean, they don't put up much of a fight and they always come out shining. But let's be realistic; not everything in life can be cleaned with good old H2O.

Let's discuss the rebellious materials that water can't stand, such as leather, electronics, suede and certain types of wood. These are akin to the "problem children" of the cleaning world.

They need special care, gentle treatment and a great deal of TLC. Water is like kryptonite to Superman for them; it can shrink, warp, discolour and essentially make their lives unbearable, and they will reward your efforts by showing you just how wrong you are.

Then, we have electronics, paper and cardboard. They can't handle water at all. One drop and they vanish. Don't even get me started on certain cleaning methods. High-pressure washer? More like high-pressure catastrophe. It's like attempting to remove a stain with a sledgehammer. Don't overlook water temperature. Using hot water on some surfaces is like pouring hot oil on a fire; it's only going to exacerbate matters.

In conclusion, while water is the all-powerful cleaner and should typically be utilised on at least approximately seventy percent of surfaces in your home, it's not completely a one-size-fits-all solution.

Some materials and situations require a more delicate touch. But hey, at least we still have vinegar and bicarbonate of soda. As with everything in life, there are techniques that work and limitations as to when to apply certain techniques.

Ask yourself how you feel about using water and microfibre cloths for cleaning now. Is it something you could consider using more of? How could this help your cleaning experience? I hope you fall in love with cleaning with water as much as me.

Which seven areas in your home could you start by cleaning with just water?

1.
2.
3.
4.
5.
6.
7.

CHAPTER TWO

Unclogging Energy

Clutter is not just the stuff on your floor, it's anything that stands between you and the life you want to be living.

PETER WALSH

The Meaning of Unclogging

I am personally intrigued by all the videos on social media about decluttering. But it occurred to me quite early on in my cleaning journey that the word "clutter" did not fully embrace the meaning of what I think we are trying to achieve. It's the action of choosing to create a space that gives us a sense of peace and luxury in our own home. It allows our energy to flow freely without unnecessary negative thoughts.

Your perspective on unclogging your home is deeply important and is directly linked to your experience of the self in your home. Let's explore this further.

I came to realise in my journey of learning to love and respect myself fully that I truly deserved to live in a space of luxury. To treasure myself also meant creating spaces in my home that facilitated my energy of being treasured and loved. Do you feel this in your home? Ask yourself what your relationship to your home is. This relationship can match what you think about yourself. If it's anything less than positive, then this chapter will help you get there. Are there any rooms that you feel do not reflect the experience you want it to create? Choose the room you feel you want to work on first.

Let's look deeper into the true art of "unclogging"—a term that goes a little deeper than simply "decluttering". Imagine it as an invisible line between your experience here and now and your living spaces.

My Realisation

One day, around ten years ago, I arrived at a client's home that was lived in by a borderline hoarder. I had been anxious for days in advance about this job.

I looked around at the stuff and things everywhere and felt truly overwhelmed and highly anxious about the task at hand and where to even begin. Everywhere I looked was stuff piled on stuff. The stench was stale and potent. What first? Do you ever have that feeling when you look into a kitchen drawer or open your closet? List the five main areas in your house that may make you feel this way:

1.
2.
3.
4.
5.
6.
7.

I felt concerned that I had been silly enough to accept this challenge. I remember the next moment so well. When I closed my eyes, took a deep breath and then opened them again, suddenly I had clarity. It occurred to me that everything around, all these things around me (the stuff), was actually very simply "energy". That's all, that simple: "energy".

Instantly my relationship to the job at hand shifted from me feeling overwhelmed by the stuff to seeing it as pure and simple energy that needed to be assessed and, where negative, removed. Simple?

Every item in your home hums with energy. Those shelves, curtains and ornaments, they're not just physical matter, they're energy in disguise. Atoms, those tiny building blocks, vibrate with life. So when you look at your favourite vase or that old chair, see beyond their form. Feel their energy: the memories, emotions and stories they hold.

Your home is *your* canvas. Within it, you wield the brush of choice. Imagine your room as a blank page waiting for your expression. With each item, you either add colour/positivity or create negativity/energy blocks within yourself. Choose wisely. When you unclog, you're not just getting rid of things; you're creating sacred space, adding a personal sense of luxury. It's where you have choice.

Suddenly the task at hand transformed turned into a clear mission. I realised that rather than asking my client what was clutter or what they did not need (a hoarder will always find a reason to keep something), there was a far more important question to ask. A question that would allow my client to let go of so many more items than they would if asked if it was needed.

Another helpful question is: "Do I really want to give my energy to continuing to cherish for it?" When you notice yourself pondering, or thinking "maybe" or "not sure", it is probably in the negative category.

I encouraged my client not to over think it. Simply put, any doubt whatsoever was a "it can go". It is simple in essence. If it's positive, i.e. brings you a feeling of happiness, joy, it's really useful, or very attractive to you., then keep it and find the right home for it.

She started to realise she did not need the "things" to keep her happy. So having released their grip, she discovered newfound lightness.

Can you ask yourself if there are any items in your home that pull you into a sense of heaviness or block your positive energy flow?

This journey with this client turned out to be such a beautiful cathartic journey between myself, the client and their stuff. She was so brave and faced a myriad of emotions letting go of things that no longer served her. In addition to this she realised her addiction to buying things that she thought she might need, just in case. It gave her the illusion that she was safe but through letting go she actually felt more truly herself and at peace with her life and her surroundings, giving her a much deeper sense of true safety and inner confidence.

Her space had enslaved her rather than feeding her with positive vibes. In letting go of this she let go of the attachment to their grief, upset and anger. This journey with my client changed everything and is the reason why I now refer to decluttering as unclogging.

My client said some interesting things after our days together unclogging her home. She felt like she had been on a long and deep journey with me as we moved around her home. It was like a spiritual journey of rediscovering her new enlivened or updated self. She felt young and free again. Look at your own home and choose a room to start the journey of unclogging.

There are various levels of unclogging needed. The less stuff in your home, the quicker this journey will be. I have listed below the different types of hoarding from very mild to severe. See which one, if any, you relate to.

Nostalgia Hoarding

Is your home like a time capsule? Crammed with relics from decades past. Old ticket stubs, broken gadgets and mismatched socks—we hoard it all. But here's the twist: hoarding isn't just about stuff. It's about memories. Each trinket holds a story, a fragment of history. Unclogging for nostalgia is the toughest of all as the fear of losing past memories can be immense and very powerful. But it can be a very powerful way of letting go of past traumas or bad experiences in one of two ways:

- Remove an item completely. Let it go so you never see it again and therefore won't trigger the negative emotion. I had a picture which I bought at a time in my life when I had lost my business and was terribly sad. I had not realised why I had felt sad being in the living room. Subconsciously, every time I went in that room it triggered that experience. Then when I decided to unclog that room, I realised that was it! That damn picture. I removed it and wow, how good that felt!
- Look at the item and rewrite history through reframing the item. I had an old ring from an old boyfriend. Every time I looked in my jewellery box and I saw that green stone ring, it subconsciously made me feel stressed as I have always been sad about losing him in my life. So I thought, *Right, I want to keep that ring,* but I reframed the experience it gave me by closing my eyes and seeing his happy face smiling at me. That made me feel so happy and now every time I see that ring I smile with happiness and gratitude for having had him in my life. It is possible to rewrite your own history.

The No-Cost Transformation

Money can't buy happiness. Remember that. Resist the urge to splurge on yet another shelf to store yet more things. Instead, explore what you already have. That old lamp? Maybe it's not just a lamp; it's a beacon of cosy evenings. That worn-out rug? It's a map of laughter and late-night conversations. Value isn't in price tags; it can also be found in old and used memories too.

Emotions

Unclogging isn't just about physical stuff; it's an emotional anchor too. Sometimes, we cling to things like barnacles on a ship. They don't fit our energy anymore, but we hesitate to let go. Consider bringing in a trusted friend—the one who sees your soul and wants the best for you. Together, you revisit memories, asking questions like, "Does this bring positivity to me?" or "Is it time to release?"

Tears: Picture this: you, sitting cross-legged amidst your belongings. The sun slants through the window, illuminating a framed photo. Tears well up. It's time. You let go—the photo, the memories, the weight. In that release, you find lightness. Your room breathes, and so do you. So, I urge you to unclog fearlessly. Choose angels over ghosts. Imagine your mind as a cluttered room. The dust settles on the shelves of your thoughts, and old memories pile up in corners. Negative emotions, like unwashed dishes, accumulate. It's easy to feel overwhelmed, suffocated by the mess. Allow yourself to let go.

Organising Emotions: Now, organise your emotions. Arrange them neatly, like books on a shelf. Label them: "gratitude", "love", "hope". When you need them, they're within reach. And when negative emotions creep in, you'll know where to find the emotional broom.

Untangling Thoughts: Untangle thoughts just as you'd tidy up a room and start unclogging your mind. Sweep away those negative thoughts that whisper doubt or fear. Sort through memories, keeping the ones that bring joy and discarding the ones that weigh you down.

Dusting Emotions: Emotions gather like dust bunnies under the bed. Acknowledge them. Sweep them out into the light. Maybe it's anger, sadness or anxiety. Dust them off, examine them and decide what to keep and what to let go.

Fresh Air and Light: Open the windows of your mind. Let in fresh air—the breeze of new perspectives. Allow sunlight to stream through, illuminating hidden corners. As you breathe, negativity dissipates, replaced by clarity and peace. Remember, just as a clean house feels lighter, so does an unclogged mind. One can't be done without the other.

Less Is More

Picture a minimalist's haven—a serene space where each item has purpose and meaning. Minimalists dance with simplicity, decluttering their lives like Marie Kondo on a caffeine high. They ask, "Does this spark joy?" Minimalism isn't just about physical possessions; it's a mindset. By shedding excess baggage (both literal and metaphorical), minimalists create room for clarity, creativity and calm. They're the Zen masters of unclogging, whispering, "Less is more." How minimalist do you consider yourself to be? Could you let go of more in your home?

OCD (Obsessive Compulsive Disorder)

On the other end of the spectrum, we find meticulous organisers—the ones who alphabetise their spice racks and colour code their sock drawers. Their mantra? "A place for everything, and everything in its place." OCD warriors thrive on precision. They unclog their mental gears by arranging their lives with surgical precision. But beware: too much order can suffocate spontaneity. Sometimes, you need a messy desk to birth brilliant ideas. People with OCD have time-consuming symptoms that can cause significant distress or interfere with daily life. Ask yourself: do I have OCD tendencies? Do I know anyone like this? The common symptoms of OCD are:

- fear of germs and dirt
- being unable to deal with uncertainty

- being obsessed with things needing to be balanced/ordered
- fear of losing control.

When unclogging I find it helpful to notice and acknowledge any of the above feelings and by doing so you can be released from their patterns.

One Step at a Time

Recently, I faced my own unclogging challenge. My bookshelves groaned under the weight of unread novels, dusty classics and guilt-inducing self-help books. I embarked on a literary quest, asking each book, "Will I read you someday?" Some whispered, "Yes, when time allows." Others screamed, "Donate me!" So, I let go. The shelves sighed in relief, and suddenly, I had room for new adventures, fresh narratives and a dash of mystery. Now on my shelf I have ten of my favourite and most meaningful books on display and I feel excited looking at them, rather than hundreds of books that made me feel stressed. Which scenario will inspire you the most? The shelf with less? Less can often allow for a richer experience.

So, where do you stand on this unclogging spectrum? Are you a minimalist, an organiser or a sentimental hoarder? Remember, unclogging isn't just about physical space; it's about reclaiming mental space. As you release what no longer serves you, you create space for growth, discovery and peace.

This year I put all my clothes aside that no longer represented my style and how I now want to present myself now. Before doing this I was overwhelmed by too many clothes whereas now I can see the clothes that inspire me and I wear something different all the time. Before I was so overwhelmed that I wore the same outfit every day!

Can you ask yourself where you are on your unclogging journey? Which spaces in your home could benefit from unclogging the most?

When Was the Last Time I Used It?

Reflect on practicality as well as positivity. If an item has been gathering dust, it might be time to reassess its place in your life as you have not needed to use it. The chances are if you have not used it for a while you don't need it at all.

Creating Space—Literally and Metaphorically

Space intrigues us. It's not just about physical room; it's mental and emotional breathing space. You are beautiful inside and out. Be brave to embrace what comes your way as a result of being open to the new.

What Obstacles Hinder Your Space Creation?

Be on the lookout for patterns of behaviour. Recognise the habits shaping your life. Some propel growth, while others hold you back. Unclogging isn't just about stuff; it's about breaking free from unhelpful patterns. Allow physical items to facilitate change in your mental wellbeing. An example, my gym room was filled with things I did not know what to do with. Every time I walked past my gym, I felt stressed. After letting go of the items I did not use (I made it into a clutter-free zone), the light came back in and I only had some inspiring pictures and my gym equipment strategically placed around the room. The bicycle was facing outside towards the trees allowing me to zoom out and get ready for the day mentally as well as physically. I adore my gym room now. It has a purpose.

Step 1: The Emotional Scan

Imagine standing in your clogged-up room. Now, let's pick a point in the top right-hand corner and rotate around your room clockwise. Chunk by chunk, top to bottom. Now with an imaginary magic wand at the ready, scan the room. As you sweep it across the space, each beep marks an energy block—a tangled necklace, a forgotten trinket or that stack of unread magazines. These items hold memories, emotions and attachments. But here's the secret: by releasing them through allowing your wand to let you know what has to go, it allows you to create space. The dusty lampshade whispers, "I've seen better days." The mismatched socks giggle, "We're soulmates, really!" And that old photo frame winks, "Remember when?" Each beep guides you—this stays, that goes. Trust your gut instinct.

Step 2: What To Keep

- Keep Pile: Here reside the items you use daily or that light up your soul. Be honest; no guilt trips allowed. If those shoes haven't seen daylight in a year, they might need a new home.
- Unclogging as Contemplation: As you declutter, you're not just tossing stuff; you're evaluating your relationship with possessions. It's like therapy for your room. Subtle changes occur—the spirit nudges the form.
- Spiritual Choreography: Unclogging isn't mere tidying; it's sacred space-making. Release old patterns and emotional cobwebs. Suddenly, your room breathes, and so do you.

Step 3: "Not Sure"

- Donate/Sell Pile: These goodies are still in the game but no longer your personal favourites. Consider donating them to charity or selling online. Imagine their second act—a new life, a fresh stage!
- Rubbish Rumba: Broken, stained, beyond-repair relics—they're like old love letters. Sentimental, yes. But guess what? You won't lose yourself by letting go. You'll gain space for new memories.
- Can't Decide: Ah, the gentle sway. Some items cling to your heart like Velcro. Pop them in the "Can't Decide" pile. Sip coffee, ponder. Maybe later, you'll be filled with clarity. Put these things in a box in a neutral space like the garage. If

after six months you have not needed or missed the items, it will be easier to let them go. Unclogging is a natural process that continually evolves like you as a beautiful being. Build in regular unclogging sessions at least every six months or every year to catch up and acknowledge your personal growth.

Organising Through "Grouping"

Organisation is a critical part to unclogging and let instinct guide you.

When I first became a professional cleaner I had never really given much thought to how to organise things in my home. I certainly had no professional experience but I quickly discovered it's a natural skill that we all have inside us.

Below I share an example of how I approached organising my wardrobe. There really is no right or wrong here. Only what works for you personally. It can depend on things such as your habits, what you use most and how you like to see colours, sizes, items, season, etc.

1. **Start to organise through grouping items first**
   - Group into categories first. Start by dividing your wardrobe into groups. T-shirts, shirts, jumpers, jackets, skirts, dresses, trousers—the whole ensemble.
   - Customise further. Maybe you want a home section, a casual corner and a formal aisle. Whatever works for you—this is your wardrobe.

- Try colour coordination. Arrange your clothes by hues. It's like curating your own rainbow. Height order is another nice touch, especially for dresses and skirts.

2. **Hang, box or drawer?**
   - Hangers: Some clothes love hanging out—literally. Hang your day-to-day favourites at eye level, particularly tailored items. They're the VIPs of your wardrobe, waving hello every morning.
   - Box/Drawer Compartments: Others prefer cosy boxes. Fold them neatly, so you can see everything you have. You'll spot them instantly when you need that specific scarf, pair of socks or beanie. I like to fold and colour code underwear, shorts, vests, ties and scarfs.

Feng Shui Your Room for Further Unclogging

Another aspect of unclogging is spotting when something is not quite right in terms of presentation.

- Picture Placement: Move that picture five inches up or to the right. *Voilà!* Your room now looks ten times better.
- Bed and Table Shuffle: Feeling adventurous? Slide your bed, twirl your kitchen table. Suddenly, your room oozes with new vibes. Trust your instincts; your room's your very own canvas.

Purpose Positivity Injection

- Future Vision: Imagine your space's future. Will it host cosy dinners, creative projects or lazy Sundays? Let the purpose of your rooms and the experiences you want to create guide your decor choices.
- Maximise Functionality: Each item should earn its keep. If it doesn't serve a purpose, it's like a party crasher. Politely escort it out.
- Home as a Living Space: Remember, your home isn't a storage unit. It's where life unfolds. Does it reflect who you are today? And who you aspire to be?

Form and Function

Let's look through this design philosophy of merging of aesthetics and purpose!

- Kitchen Utensils: A chef's knife. Its purpose? Precision. It slices, dices and pirouettes through veggies. The handle? Like a velvet glove—comfortable, confident. Beauty? It's in the seamless choreography of form and function.
- Architectural *Pas de Deux*: Picture a building—a safe space for life's events. Natural light shining through windows, shading twirls with eaves. Cross ventilation meets with fresh air. It's the sturdy partner, keeping temperatures steady. Aesthetic and function.

- Machinery: Ovens, mixers, grinders—they're the divas of functionality. An oven preheats like a soprano hitting high notes. A mixer kneads dough with rhythmic precision. And that grinder? It grinds meat to the perfect tempo. Beauty? It's in their harmonious performance.

Design can inspire us to be better human beings and change our home positively. Think carefully and deliberately before buying something new and consider its design and how the design complements your space.

Connecting Philosophy to Decluttering

- Zen Mindfulness: Unclogging isn't just about tossing stuff; it's Zen in action. Mindfulness is awareness of each possession's purpose. Does it speak to you in your life's story?
- Non-Attachment: Like a Zen master, we appreciate beauty without clinging. Sentimental relics? They're like delicate notes. We release them, creating space for new melodies.

So, let form follow function, let beauty have purpose. And may your decluttered space give you peace.

The Impact of Trauma on Clutter and Hoarding

Upon experiencing trauma, it's possible we become withdrawn, fatigued and somewhat adrift. Hoarding can take root in this context. We are prone to forming attachments to items similarly to the way we attach to people or pets. Such attachments can become problematic in the aftermath of a traumatic incident. We seek anything that offers safety, even if it means submerging ourselves in material possessions. Another trauma-induced tendency is to acquire items we don't require. Ever found yourself ordering items on online under the illusion of their usefulness, only to confine them to the back of a cupboard? This cycle can persist until our dwellings are swamped with unused objects.

Letting Go in Times of Grief

Relinquishing material possessions does not equate to releasing your grip on a departed loved one. But how do we let go?

Grief is one of life's most painful experiences. The demise of a cherished one can activate an inner mechanism of fear—the fear of losing everything and never retrieving it.

The correlation between loss and hoarding is often linked to the belongings of the deceased, or items that remind us of them. I once counselled a woman who couldn't part with the dress she wore when she discovered her son's passing. Although it represented her most traumatic memory, she preserved it in a sealable bag on her wardrobe's top shelf. She staunchly resisted the idea of giving away any of her son's possessions: his clothing, paperwork, even his bed frame and mattress. In such sensitive cases, allow yourself extra time to process these items and exhibit compassion towards yourself.

So, how do we internalise the idea that parting with these items is acceptable? Firstly, understand that releasing the belongings of a lost loved one doesn't eradicate their memory. Secondly, approach this daunting task with self-compassion. Don't feel guilty about keeping some items. Lastly, avoid pressuring yourself—don't impose deadlines or strive to discard everything at once.

Overcoming Financial Hardship and Its Clinging Effect

Financial hardship as another experience can induce behaviours akin to wartime rationing, tight budgeting and retention of unnecessary items. We "baby boomers" mostly have parents and grandparents with wartime memories. Clinging to possessions becomes yet another trauma response. We fear that once these items vanish, we'll never be able to replace them.

I once assisted a woman who, following a turbulent divorce and left with three young children and a hefty mortgage, felt desperate. She aimed to save money in any way possible, storing her children's clothes for reuse, and impulsively buying items from charity shops, only to forget them in a cupboard later. Even after stabilising her finances, she remained attached to this stuff, the lingering trauma still influencing her behaviour. She clung to the notion that she might need these items one day, despite them being stowed away, lost and forgotten.

Kindness in Decluttering: A Necessary Approach

As we embark on decluttering following our trauma responses, we must do so with kindness. Our minds have conditioned us to believe these items were our allies during tough times, and they may represent fragments of our identities, regardless of their actual value. Discarding items, whether they hold sentimental worth or are simply "I'll use this one day" items, can be challenging if these objects become part of your trauma response. However, releasing some of these items can certainly offer a sense of liberation and healing. Every item in your home occupies space. The more items present, the greater the surface area requiring cleaning, and consequently, more time spent on the task. I consistently stress this point to those whose abundance of possessions makes achieving a tidy home in a reasonable timeframe physically unfeasible.

The Gratitude Ritual

Acknowledge the emotional weight tied to possessions. By expressing gratitude for their past role, you honour their significance while freeing yourself.

In the corner of my room sits a lamp—a relic from a sun-kissed adventure in Thailand. Its base, smooth as polished stone, carries the weight of memories. My best friend gifted it to me, whispering, "May it light your nights, even when oceans separate us."

- I touch the lamp, tracing its curves. It feels heavy, substantial. Like love, it anchors me.
- I'm grateful—for friendship, for shared laughter under Thai lanterns, for whispered secrets in moonlit bungalows.

Medals of a Silent Journey with a Hoarder

One of my clients who was a self-proclaimed hoarder was facing a dilemma when we got to sorting out her cherished office. She had previously been a psychiatric nurse in her younger years.

As is often the way with hoarders, she was incredibly bright. There were boxes filled to the roof with old patient records. We could hardly get into the room. There was also a lifelong trail of post received through her lifetime. Everything from junk mail through to meaningful letters from friends and families.

In her dusty drawers lay her notes—scribbles from the past fifty years at least. They were her medals, earned silently, of memories and interactions. You see, growing up with multiple disabilities, she felt she lacked tangible achievements. No sports trophies, no art accolades. But these notes? They were her secret victories.

This was the hardest and most emotionally charged room to do. We had to come up with an approach that would allow her to cherry pick the memories and documents and cherish the most meaningful and cherished memories.

We stepped back and I asked her, "What does this room make you feel and see?" She said stressed, inquisitive, tired. It looks messy, overwhelming, dirty.

I asked her, "What would you like to feel and see when you walk into this room?" She said, "I would like to be able to see the floor, see the light come through the window again, see the room as a showcase of my life's work, to be able to reminisce with friends and family."

So, we came up with an approach.

We grouped things into categories of what we were likely to find:

- work files
- friends' letters
- family letters
- cookery books
- non-fiction books
- photos
- pens/paper/envelopes (all stationery)
- magazines
- random items including gifts and ad hoc purchases

I asked her then what would she like doing with the above groups and this is what we came up with:

- Work folders were to be put away in boxes categorised by the year they related to. Until she was ready to let them go, they would be stored neatly in the locked garage.
- Friends' and family letters were put in a box for her to sort through. She came up with the idea of green lever arch folders for friends and pink for family and then again divided by years.
- Cookery books were to be kept and displayed in height order on the top shelves.
- Non-fiction books were kept on the second shelf down.
- Photos were to be found and put in boxes for her to sift through and display in albums. We bought ten for her to get going.
- All stationery was sifted through and put in boxes. We found over thirty-five staplers and hole punchers. A symptom of repeat buying when you can't find things. Spares to be given to charity.
- Magazines were put into type, date and edition groups on shelves.
- Random items were put in boxes for her to sift through and she put in charity boxes all usable unwanted items.

We then discussed how she would feel if this was achieved? She said, "I am excited to be able to see and find old treasure and memories."

Then we discussed the elephant in the room. This is the most important conversation to have when helping a hoarder or when sorting personal things that have accumulated over years. If she was to go through every paper and item herself, it would probably take more than a year to sift through. This would never feasibly be possible. So I asked her to trust me and give me permission to put random things into the following three categories:

Rubbish: By rubbish we mean things that have absolutely no use to anyone because they are unfixable. Like a torn used envelope or a broken pen. Any items I was not sure about, again I put separately into another large box for her to go through.

Sentimental: I explained that nothing I found that may fall into the following categories would be thrown away to allow her to ponder over in her own time:

- Fixer-Uppers: Some notes are torn, ink fading, with promises to fix them, like broken wings.
- Just-in-Case Scribbles: Others—ideas, dreams—kept "just in case". They're a safety net, a "what if".
- Promised Potentials: "Once I learn more." These notes held promises—to herself, to the universe.
- Too-Good-to-Throw-Aways: Sentences that shimmered, paragraphs that sang. Too precious to discard.
- Broken Fragments: Some notes are literal fragments—half-thoughts, scribbled in haste, unfinished stories, leafing through them, like a time traveller. Each note whispers, "You were here."

Going through any of the above and considering letting go is a scary proposition for any hoarder and needs to be faced. We discussed the fact that yes, maybe I might throw away something she might well have felt she needed. But to look at the price of *not* doing so.

If we leave it as it is she will never be able to find anything. If we go ahead with this process she would re-find joy in her possessions yet again.

She decided after much deliberation and conversation that it was a small price to pay. Every time during this process, when she got anxious we reminded each other of this fact, took a deep breath, felt the wave of the emotion and then I would support her to let it go. You cannot expect to go through a process like this without being faced with anxiety, anger or upset. But now, I detach. I honour things and their silent journey, their role in my growth. And I release them, like paper boats on a river.

After three days of intensive sorting we got there. Now this is an extreme example but the process will be a similar one however large or small the project. Remember, my fellow memory keeper, decluttering isn't just about space; it's about honouring the past while creating room for new stories.

Light streamed again through unclogged windows. She slept better, dreamt of open fields, not crowded rooms. Her heart, too, unclogged. She described the feeling that she felt her husband's presence again, not as a weight, but as a gentle breeze—a reminder to live, to let go.

This remarkable women also shared a story since of when her grand children came around to visit and they notice the photo albums. They all sat down at the table and went through the pictures inquisitively asking questions about her life. Her grandchildren would have never received these rich stories of generations soon to be lost, if it was not for the unclogging process. These photos would have gone on lost forever.

A Little More About Rubbish

Last but not least, when unclogging we need to explore what rubbish is exactly.

Is it filthy? Broken? Unusable, no longer working? No longer needed? Think about the amount of waste in landfills. Things exist because all things are related to each other. The people and things in life make you who you are. In the Buddhist culture they say it's not for you to judge whether something is useful or not, or designate things to rubbish that you no longer want and treat as rubbish.

It's not just about judging if something is useful or not, it's also about embodying a spirit of gratification towards physical items.

Buddhists also believe people who do not respect the physical universe and the things in it don't respect people. Within any physical object much time and effort was put into it. The spirit of the person who made it. I remember when I was young and sitting in my bedroom when trying to get to sleep. I was looking at every single item, from the door handle to the doll, to the light to the glass, imagining how many people were involved in making each item and the story behind the making of everything… from the idea to the design, to the making, to the transporting, to the selling and then the buying and transporting to be here now with me. It used to blow my mind away and I would feel humbled as to how much energy must have gone into even getting a door handle for my home. It made me feel so grateful.

I am not suggesting we keep everything in endless cupboards in space we don't have but some things, despite being used or old, might have some life left in them somewhere else and have the opportunity to shine yet again. So it's important in all this when unclogging to remember to appreciate the things you do have. Friends, charity shops and online selling are all wonderful ways to give things another life in a new context.

Cycle of Housekeeping

Unclog: Buddhist monks live with simple surroundings and have minimal possessions that all have their place. Try and really be true to what you actually need to bring beauty, joy and ease to your life.

Group: It's impossible to do a good tidy when things are not grouped together in their correct categories, e.g. get all the pens scattered around the house into one container in the office. Everything belongs somewhere and has a purpose of being aesthetically pleasurable or needed and has a useful function.

Tidy: Once everything is grouped and placed in the right rooms it's time to ensure all items are tidy and placed for easy access and with pleasure to look at.

Clean: Put daily, weekly, monthly and seasonal cleaning routines in place for your home.

CHAPTER THREE

Chunk by Chunk
(Step by Step)

It takes as much energy to wish as it does to plan.

ELEANOR ROOSEVELT

The Key to Success: Little Steps. Focus on Progress, Not Perfection

Good fortune is what happens when progress meets opportunity. Part of the process of preparation facilitates you to notice the opportunities as they arrive in your life. This is what we call serendipity. Through discovering my five principles I discovered how to be a successful cleaner and through mastering this I discovered this foundation as a metaphor for all areas in my life. I would now call myself successful. Why am I now able to call myself successful? It's down to this simple act that I learnt through cleaning.

Many people get daunted by the thought of cleaning a whole home. Some of our deep house cleaning projects require hundreds of hours. The thought of it can be daunting. Can you relate to this?

I remember cracking the first big house and how elated I was. I chose a point at the top of the house high up. It was a Victorian house with very tall windows and I suddenly got it. I visualised my top point high up to the top right-hand corner and wiped the top right-hand side of the inside window and worked my way down to the skirting board and then chose the next chunk, top to bottom.

I kept repeating this until the whole room had been cleaned and eventually arrived at my starting point. Wow, that was satisfying! If you look at the room as a whole it can be daunting. Being a domestic goddess is being fearless. Nothing overwhelms you because we follow a step-by-step process. This became a metaphor for life. Now when I run my business and my life as a domestic goddess I break down all areas of my life that I want to grow in and am responsible for.

So, for example, as part of running my business I break it down into areas I am responsible for such as:

- business growth
- marketing
- personnel
- legal
- finance
- operations
- training

Then I break down at least one mini step I want to make each day. This simple act enabled me to build a robust million pound cleaning business within two years.

I did the same with running my home. Here are some examples of areas of running a home:

- washing
- drying
- ironing
- cleaning bathrooms
- cleaning kitchen

- cleaning bedroom
- cleaning reception rooms
- bed making
- cooking
- restocking consumables
- tidying
- de-cobwebbing
- inside windows
- outside windows
- gutter cleaning
- gardening

By doing mini steps each day every day I feel and breathe progress—that's what makes us powerful and strong. Contrary to belief it's not always about being perfect.

In my menopause journey I have been doing simple arm exercises daily—five minutes only—and now I have toned arms and can wear short T-shirts again.

What areas of your life bug you a little? Are there any areas where you would like to be more the version of you you feel proud of? Pick just three things and monitor daily baby steps. And within three months you will have that sense of pride: I DID IT! I often wonder if the problem in this fast paced world is we expect instant gratification therefore sometimes losing the art of gradual progress and life.

How I Came to the Chunk-by-Chunk Realisation

Twenty years on, I clearly remember my first professional clean like it was yesterday, which is crazy as my general memory is absolutely dreadful. The job came following a planned week of leaflet dropping in my local area in Cheltenham. My two sons of four and five years old (at the time) sons were in tow helping me hand out leaflets.

They told anyone who dare listen what a great cleaner I was! Within one week I was fully booked. I could not believe it. My first property was an end of terrace house. It looked small on the outside but my goodness it was like a TARDIS.

Inside I was terrified by the challenge as I had no professional experience. I looked around to see if there was a domestic cleaning professional course and found none so I decided to brace it and find the courage within me to find a way and learn. Of course this would have to be done by trial and error if I wanted to become the very best in the industry.

I did panic inside as I had no idea what the plan should be or how long a clean should, or even would, take me. Do you ever wonder how long it should take to clean your own home?

I remember cleaning the first toilet like it was yesterday. I think it was the first time I had ever had to look at the detail of how a toilet was manufactured. Little did I know that this moment would lead to my fourth cleaning principle of "zooming in" which we cover in the next chapter.

The toilet seat hinges were a fiddle and the outer bowl looked like it had never been cleaned and was covered in yellow stained grime.

I had not discovered microfibre cloths at that point. I drenched the whole toilet in bleach (plus my clothing) with a non-porous J-cloth and then kitchen rolls to dry off the residue bleach. I went through rolls and rolls of kitchen roll.

You don't need to be a mathematician to work out I was losing money and was not at all eco-friendly. Within months of cleaning like this my asthma hit me badly and I was wheezing badly all day. I am convinced it was from inhaling bleach and harsh cleaning products.

Have you ever inhaled strong cleaning products? What must it be doing do our health?

The only thing going for me at that stage was my desire to do a good job. My heart was in the right place but that was about it at this stage.

Even to this day it's not always easy to estimate how long things will take. But a simple rule of thumb is the more "things" in the house, the longer it takes as each "thing" takes up space and becomes something else that needs to be cleaned. Which is why we explored unclogging in the last chapter.

When I go and assess how long a client's house clean will take I will look at the items and imagine each item as part of a surface to be cleaned. In very cluttered houses the workload can be increased by more than 300 percent.

To clean the "things" alone could easily be three times larger than the total of house surfaces alone. So the unclogging chapter before is not just essential for our spiritual life but also for the practical aspects of allocating the correct amount of time to clean the house and if indeed it is at all possible to keep on top of, with daily, weekly, monthly and seasonal cleaning sessions.

As a rule of thumb a typical bedroom should take around twenty minutes if it's been unclogged, but can take over an hour to clean properly if there lots of things around. In turn, getting motivated to clean a room with lots of things in it is daunting, so by return they get left and we are in a vicious circle of it just collecting more and more dust.

Scatter Gun Cleaning

In all truth, in my early days I was a scatter gun cleaner. I would look in panic at what I had to do and picked the thing that looked the dirtiest... or the least depending on my energy and intention levels to get the job done.

Many of my clients describe how they spend so much of their energy thinking about what they should be cleaning and feeling resistance to doing it. Do you ever feel this way in your own home and fall foul to this approach?

As a general rule of thumb, and to know you are on the right track it should take the following amount of time to clean a home:

Five plus hours on a five bed plus
Four hours in a four bed house
Three hours in a three bed house
Two and a half hours in a two bed house
Two hours in a one bed house

Separating Deep Cleaning Items from General Cleaning

I remember one of my first mistakes was starting off with a filthy oven. I ended spending the whole allocated time cleaning that. Quite rightly my client was disappointed as he wanted to come back to a clean home and ended up with a clean oven. I have since learnt to put aside things like a filthy oven (this is a "special project") and manage expectations better. Areas that need deep cleaning need to be approached differently and separately to a general clean.

My aim is to achieve a clean home that is always being rotated so you never need to get to the place where deep cleaning is required. I make sure every time I use my oven I give it a quick wipe out and it never gets to the stage where it needs a really deep clean.

Chunk-by-Chunk Discovery

After my first year of cleaning as a professional, I discovered the chunk-by-chunk, top-to-bottom method. Quite by mistake. I went to visit my grandmother who gave me this advice and I have never looked back. I recall sharing my challenges with her and she excitingly said to me that when she went to school they studied "Domestic Science".

So to summarise, the most hygienic and logical way to clean is to start top down. We all know this makes sense because in general gravity causes matter to fall downwards. (Imagine cleaning a table and then knocking all the dust and cobwebs from the ceiling onto it.)

The day I learnt that and gave it a go—the missing link in the chain stopping me from being an amazing cleaner—it took the stress away 100 percent from cleaning and I just focused on what was in front of me and cleaned step by step, chunk by, top to bottom.

Likewise the thought of a long car journey and getting there can be daunting, but if you simply follow the directions road by road you get there just fine. In my early days I was nervous that using my damp, dry, buff technique on each area chunk by chunk, top to bottom would take too long, but to my delight it worked a dream. I moved my way around rooms swiftly and efficiently! It worked and my clients were delighted with my achievements.

I did not have to think of all of the hundreds of items that needed cleaning but to just do the wet, dry, buff technique described in chapter one with what was in front of me. I stopped feeling overwhelmed. I felt like I was a woman with a plan and a purpose. Cleaning each item and surface as I moved around the room became exciting and all absorbing!

Larger items like ovens, special deep clean items, could be addressed separately and allowed me to keep on top of houses as effectively as possible.

Do you find yourself being overwhelmed by the jobs you have in your mind that need doing? Try following this chunk-by-chunk, top-to-bottom process and separate out deep cleaning jobs as separate projects to attack when you have the energy.

The Process

If you are tired of spending hours cleaning your home only to realise that the dust and cobwebs on the ceiling have now rained down onto surfaces you just cleaned, and all the other accumulated detritus of life, well, have no fear! There's a fearless solution to this never-ending cycle of cleaning, and it's called the chunk-by-chunk, top-to-bottom process.

Picture this. You walk into a room with your cleaning tools in hand, and instead of immediately diving into scrubbing the floor, you march straight to the corner of the room that is the highest up and closest to the heavens. And, just like a ninja, you strike with your duster, preferably a microfibre cloth, and conquer that vertical space of about five feet, with great satisfaction and no thought for personal survival. So pick a corner and that's your starting point.

Once that area is spotless, you move on to the next section of the wall, and the next and so on, working your way from top to bottom like a boss. This method is like a game of Tetris (I only know this because one of my sons has it on his computer), where you have to clear the top row before it gets too cluttered.

Starting with the ceiling is like hitting the jackpot because dust and cobwebs love to collect up there. Most spiders and other creatures know that they can collect more up there and it's the safest place for a home. For those in some parts of the country this can be a major issue! So, grab a long-handled duster with a microfibre cloth tied round the end with a step ladder, and get ready to take back the Donbas territory. Because let's be realistic, who wants to spend their time cleaning only to have to do it again a few days later because the dust settled back down? With this technique, your cleaning will be done in no time knowing that your effort will make a huge difference!

The moral of this tale is clean like a boss, from the top down. Always!

Remove Items

In order to clean surfaces it's key to move items first before cleaning a surface. Depending on what's in from of you, you can move items from a particular chunk to the left or the right. Clean the surfaces, then the items, then return them. As I return items I make sure they are beautifully positioned for beauty and aesthetics. In bathrooms I group items and place them in height order, labels at the front. Now you will understand why principle two "unclogging and grouping" is essential groundwork to do before cleaning.

The Four Steps

Also this chunk-by-chunk approach became a great metaphor for my life and I have broken down four things I do as part of the chunk-by-chunk process.

1. Have a Goal

It could be to make the house clean and ordered so I feel uplifted and relaxed when I come home from work. It could be to declutter my wardrobe. I advise to pick a goal that is doable and not to be too overambitious otherwise we might end up giving up and then beating ourselves up for not achieving.

Far better to be clear about what you want to achieve and let go of trying to conquer the world in a day! Accept what can't be done and schedule in chunk by chunk in doable timeframes. This way we can build on our successes in our home and feel proud of our achievements. As much as I advocate a spick and span house, give yourself a little slack so you can put aside time for building quality memories and experiences in your home too.

2. Zoom In with Your Eyes and Look at What You Are Doing

This will bring you into the here and now and help you feel present and alive. One of the reasons I fell in love with cleaning is this process. Through doing this I literally get transported into the moment and I am fully absorbed in what is right in front of me.

I arrive at my destination of a clean home with a sense of peace and no sense of negative resistance. Do you think that when cleaning you can focus with intention on what you are physically doing right in front of you?

This is the skill results in us experiencing , "Cleaning is so therapeutic." All our problems go away and at the end of it you have clean spaces to allow life's journey to flow more freely—right through you. If you feel a little pessimistic ask yourself, "Can I give this a try?" Like meditation, the more you practise it, the deeper you become at one with the world. This is why I feel I am the luckiest person in the word with this job. You will also come to appreciate your intentions more and more.

3. Breathe In and Out and Accept What's in Front of You

Accept whatever dirt is in front of you. Getting upset, angry or resentful won't change anything. I think none of us are exempt from having mini tantrums in life. It goes without saying that the only person you are hurting is yourself in these moments (along with anyone else on the brunt of the outburst).

It really is true when we say negativity creates negativity and positivity creates positivity. As I get wiser, I become better at being more constructive when facing the dirt that "should" have been cleaned last weekend or the washing up left in the sink.

Dirt build-up is something that happens to us all like birth, death, sunlight, moonlight, taxes. We can't change it. So through acceptance I have grown to see my cleaning as an act of love and respect. People who choose to ignore it and don't pull their own weight could be called on it with love and respect. Through looking after your home you are showing respect to yourself.

The more love and respect we show ourselves, the more we will feel at peace with yourself. Can you show yourself more love and respect in your own home? And how will this make a difference to your life on a daily basis?

4. Have the Discipline to Follow Chunk by Chunk, Top to Bottom

You will find your inner flow. Anything that needs to be deep cleaned will hinder your flow, so put it aside for now as a deep cleaning project. Get into your rhythm with your damp, dry, buff technique. The key is to cover the surfaces chunk by chunk. Cheating does not work. If you skip areas, your home does not get the full body clean it deserves. You will know what you have missed and the sense of satisfaction and knowing it's done will not be quite the same as a full job done.

What Do We Mean by "Finding Your Flow"?

I want to explore this idea of finding your inner flow more.

At times in my life I have felt all I was doing was reacting to problem after problem. Nothing worked. My negativity seemed to be attracting more negativity and I even resorted to antidepressants to try to change my dark depressed feelings. Have you ever felt like this or know someone who feels this way?

I soon learnt that, through cleaning, all I needed was a goal and then the desire and courage to take baby steps towards achieving the goal and that then in turn I would find my flow. So to summarise, my magic steps to find my inner flow are as follows:

- Have a goal
- Have the desire/courage to be present
- Accept what's in front of me
- Have the discipline to follow the chunk-by-chunk process

Mini Steps Lead to Big Changes

But what makes the flow happen? It's partly when the inner resistance has gone. Let me try to explain a recent experience where I found my flow. Last year I put on a lot of weight and my hips started aching. I increased my painkillers and stayed in bed working all day from bed. I was getting more and more unhealthily overweight and dependent on painkillers.

I was depressed by how I looked and felt. One morning I remember waking up and I said to myself, "I have had enough." Life felt so dark I thought things could not get any worse.

I decided I would do some daily exercise, eat good food and stop drinking alcohol. Day one, I put on my running shoes. I tried to run but quickly got out of breath. So I decided to do *something*. I trusted that *something* was better than nothing, right?

I didn't ask myself what I can't do (which was certainly not run for half an hour) but I asked my body what it could do. It came to me. Run ten steps then walk ten steps. I did one lap of the park in ten minutes.

I got home and felt a little bit proud of myself that at least I did *something*. I made myself some healthy soups and ensured I was nourished. When I was hungry, I ate a little more soup. That night I said I did not need a drink to take away the emotional pain and help me sleep.

Within one week my heart rate dropped literally (checked on my Fitbit). I almost immediately felt less anxious and depressed. Admittedly I woke up a bit in the night but it allowed me to start thinking about the changes I could make to my life and how I could in turn work on myself, my business, my home and life in general.

The next day I gave myself a goal of two laps of the park and each day I pushed myself a little more. I started to feel more positive and found my inner flow. Within five months of mini progressions daily I was running eight kilometres a day, fitting into clothes I loved and finding my inner flow. My passion for life. Naturally when I do the right things, I am a loving and positive person. When you do the right things by you what are your own unique beautiful qualities? Are you adventurous, thoughtful, kind, funny, loving?

Like life in general, cleaning must be done systematically. Pick a high-up area in one corner of your room. Go top to bottom, chunk by chunk. I quickly learnt to start high up dusting and de-cobwebbing, then the walls top down, then to surfaces, surface fronts and finally the floor base and skirting boards.

Here's a small but powerful point: open windows where possible to allow fresh air in to replace stale air. Cleanliness is not just about what we can see with our naked eye.

We don't always know what will happen in life. Go with life's flow, its twists and turns, and if it's not as you want it, adjust it slightly. Little micro adjustments allow you to flow with more trust in life. Life wants to be lived, right here, right now. Like a sailing boat, you go in zigzags against the wind to get to your destination. Life is not just one straight line.

The Unknown

When you get into cleaning your home, we don't always know what we are going to face when we open that closet. I know so many clients who describe that they feel like they just want to change their whole house but can't face it because it's too big a task. They feel overwhelmed. Have you ever felt that in your own home or in life in general?

I remember being told about flow many times when struggling to learn a new skill such as dressage or driving a car.

I clearly remember an incident on a cold autumn morning when my horse-riding instructor shouted at me to stop getting overwhelmed with all the technical instructions. She said forget all that!

She and I were getting particularly frustrated in trying to teach my horse to do an extended trot. I was getting more and more frustrated with myself to the point of tears.

She then shouted, "Forget what I am telling you to do and just go with the flow."

I clearly remember taking a deep breath and just letting go. I found my flow and the extended trot just happened.

The same happened to me when learning to drive a car. Sure, you have to learn many things such as how to turn the wheel, change gear, read the road signs, adjust your speed appropriately, etc. But there comes a point where you need to let go and allow yourself to go with the flow to enable yourself to let your instincts fall into place.

I have had many moments where "finding my flow" has been empowering and exciting. Every time I clean a house it is another opportunity to find my flow and transform my living space.

Many people say being a cleaner is an unskilled job for people that are not clever enough to do something more worthy. I disagree. I think it's an integral part of life to maintain a home that supports who you are and where you want to get to. Ask yourself which parts of your home support you and which parts need working on?

A Cleaning Challenge

Going back to the beginning of my career as a cleaner, I remember arriving at my third client's home. It had three floors, two large Alsatians, three cats, and the downstairs was covered with copious balls of hair everywhere.

There were filthy toddler toys all over the floors, fingerprints on the inside of the walls and windows, smelly nappies in bins, kitchen surfaces covered in filthy items and unwashed cutlery. Black sinks and smelly drains. Damp towels on bathroom floors and bad odours coming out of toilet bins. Toothpaste all over the sinks. Toilets full of goodness knows what and the list goes on. I truly felt overwhelmed.

But I remember that moment and I took a deep breath and I picked a corner and started working my way around the room, cleaning whatever was in front of me without judgement. I got immersed into the moment and fell in love with transforming what was in front of me.

Being a cleaner teaches you to be non-judgemental to yourself first and then, in turn, others. I was always surprised when interviewing for new staff and I always ask what they like and do not like about cleaning.

I have often heard in response they hate it when clients "live like pigs" or "leave the washing up for me to do".

To be a great cleaner, I believe, is to not judge our clients for what they leave for us to do, or how they live. Our job is to clean their home and to give them that sense of space and joy being in their own home. That in turn often helps your client experience a shift and perspective on life and even can give them the kickstart motivation they need to keep on top of things and a space that reflects who they want to be.

Negative Thoughts (What I Call "Noise")

I am not the thoughts in my head, the noise. It's not the higher me talking. Likewise through viewing any negative thoughts (about myself or my client for not having the well-organised kitchen or wardrobe) simply as noise, it allows me to be free, get absorbed into the task and feel the flow.

I liken feeling the flow as demonstrating pure unadulterated love.

I have moved many clients to tears through helping them transform their home. Some people just need that push and support to fall back in love with their home and in turn themselves. Creating space and beauty in your home in turn seems to create space in your life for joy and new experiences.

By the time I finished my first kitchen, I was moved by the transformation in front of me. I didn't need a degree to do this. I didn't need to be smart or clever. All I had to do was go chunk by chuck and be brave enough to go with the flow.

I realised that actually if I truly want to grow and achieve in life all I had to do was embrace what was in front of me and do the do. It was an enlightening moment which I keep reliving day by day. This brings me hope and joy.

Be Brave When "Bad" Things Happen

This learning has transformed my business and personal life also. Before I had this realisation I would panic and feel a victim of circumstances and possibly even blame someone else. Now I trust the flow of life and work out a plan for the next steps (or micro steps) I need to take to solve the problem rather than have a tantrum or push my toys out of the pram.

Nine times out of ten all I need to do to solve a problem is to respond and action the next mini step to resolve the issue. Then funnily enough something incredible happens and I realise that actually, for example, losing that client was for a reason and brought serendipity into my life. I am less fearful now and feel braver than ever. Let my life take me somewhere by following the flow.

I love this AA prayer. I feel it's applicable to me in all areas of my life:

> *Grant me the serenity to accept the things I cannot change, the courage to change the things I can and the wisdom to know the difference.*

We all need to find our flow, our desire in life. Life wants to be lived. Go with the flow and let go of trying to judge what's in front of you. Be courageous and move through whatever we face and stop judging life and criticising what's in front of you. That won't change anything.

Finally, when facing each chunk I look at it like this:

1. **Make the task a little harder and perhaps challenge yourself.** Say, for example, I get to the coffee machine. When I first started cleaning, I would just wipe the outside of it. Now I challenge myself to go further.

2. **Break the task into sub-tasks.** I realised to do an even better job I should break it down into sub-tasks, such as the water

container, the coffee pod deposit area, the water overflow container, etc.

3. **Be in the moment**. Watch the process of transformation right in front of your eyes. Breathe in, breathe out.

4. **Finish the task to perfection**. Get right into the detail. Don's leave and say it's good enough. Build on this. This reminds me of *The Karate Kid* movie (1984), "Wax on, wax off." Breathe in, breathe out. Keep following the next chunk, top to bottom.

Save Time—Clean Like a Pro

This is my favourite benefit. When driving, you look ahead at the road, read the surfaces, read the possible hazards, and correct the use of your feet, hands and navigation to move through space. At the beginning, it takes immense focus. The more experience you gain using the water, the cloth and follow the chunk-by-chunk process on different surfaces, the more efficient and more confident you will become. And the more effortless driving the car becomes. You become a professional.

I remember when I passed my driving test on my eighteenth birthday I planned a trip to Paris. I was terrified but I remember thinking all I had to do was follow the map, one road to the next road. This helped me feel less daunted. It was the same with cleaning. I remember the day I realised all I had to do was create my own road map when cleaning.

Finding Courage

My father was shocked that for my first journey after passing my driving test was a drive to Paris. Back in my late teens I was fearless. Since those years, through many life experiences, I began to believe that being fearless and courageous was a dangerous thing.

It is only now in the later part of my life, and through being a cleaner, I am relearning to have courage again, by breaking down my goals into mini steps or bite-sized chunks. As a result I am re-finding my flow and the courage and love that we are all born with.

As a result I saved time from my scatter gun cleaning approach going back on myself again and again and losing the anxiety of "have I done everything?".

The marvellous byproduct of this was, while cleaning chunk by chunk top to bottom, when I came across something that was particularly filthy (an oven, for example) I would leave that to the end and if I had the time I would do it. If I did not have the time I would contact the client and explain that I noticed it needed doing and would they like me to come back for an extra two hours to get it cleaned. This was a win-win for me. Like it can be a win-win for you. I got the whole house done but a special project of cleaning the oven was identified and the client felt happy that I cared and offered a solution.

If you follow the chunk-by-chunk process using mainly water in at least seventy percent of your home, you will soon be cleaning like a pro without even thinking about it.

The other important thing about the chunk-by-chunk process is knowing when your cloth, one or two wipes per square footage, is needed. Do not over-clean an area or you will be there for many unnecessary hours.

Top to Bottom, Chunk by Chunk

Taking things step by step is used in therapy, meditation and even massage. You pinpoint your starting point, your middle and your end and work through them. This allows your mind to process what it is you're doing, creating order. When applied in therapy we start by sharing our troubles, which in cleaning can be assessing your space.

The therapist will then pinpoint the area they feel most needs looking at and from there they will work their way through these, creating a sequence and allowing our minds to work through these issues in a much more structured way.

It is the same when related back to cleaning. This structure when applied means picking a starting point and working our way around a room from left to right or right to left going from top to bottom. Perfection can only come from order!

The first good idea you might have is to go and have a cup of coffee to think hard about how you might avoid doing it all!

Without a plan you might not do it or suddenly there are other more important priorities to attend to. A common complaint I get from clients is that they never seem to have the time even when allocating a weekend to do it. Then the stress of *not* doing it compounds the feelings and relationship to cleaning.

What is your relationship to cleaning? Do any of the below negative emotional statements resonate with you in relationship to cleaning your own home? Don't claim you want an amazing home and then run away from the growing pains.

Pride: It won't make a difference to me anyway. I have more important things to do. Cleaning is just a chore and someone else should do it for me

Anger: Why is it always left to me? No one else takes responsibility. There are not enough hours in the day to do this on top of other more important things in life

Fear: It's overwhelming and impossible to achieve in the time I have available. I just can't achieve anything in the time I have available.

Upset. It's overwhelming. I wish someone would love me and help me. I am all alone.

Apathy. I don't have the right equipment to do the job. I am just too tired to do anything.

We all have our fair share of negative feelings when it comes to cleaning, and life's challenges in general but I promise you, by following the chunk-by-chunk method these emotions will be conquered.

When you finish, you can step back, admire your work and give yourself a pat on the back for a job well done.

Pacing

Approach cleaning like driving a car. Go too fast and you will likely have an accident but calm-paced cleaning gets you there quicker. It will also be enjoyable.

I liken this to how the tortoise beat the hare. The moral of the story being consistent and steady wins the race.

There would be no use in rushing around trying to get everything done at once. This would cause you to do lots of jobs quickly but badly. Much the same as multi-tasking, even the most professional jugglers have their limits.

Instead, take a few moments to assess and prioritise, then use your time, taking a note of areas that need extra attention. This will go a long way into pacing yourself and using your time more wisely.

Readiness Score

Another aspect of getting a house ready is to go for what I call a "house readiness score". Like on a Fitbit, I have a readiness score based on sleep and exercise quality. It tells me how ready I am to face the day.

I have my own list and I run through it weekly. As you move around your house, make sure you get a sense of completion, the icing on the cake for a satisfaction score! It also avoids no end of frustration in the house when things aren't where they should be on a busy or stressful morning.

Harmony in the home is everything and a little weekly preparation goes a long way. Can you write your own weekly checklist? Think of all the things that cause stress if not handled. I bet you love a calm home just like me.

Here are some examples of what I mean by "house readiness score":

Kitchen

Has the washing up been put away?
Has the dishwasher been emptied?
Is there enough milk for the week?
Are there enough coffee pods?
Are out-of-date items removed from the fridge?
Do we have enough soap/washing liquid/dishwasher tablets/bin bags?

Office

Are the pencils in the jar sharpened?

Do pens have lids?

Do I have replacement ink for the printer?

Is my shredder/bin empty?

Wardrobe

Are your shirts ready to wear and ironed?

Have the clean clothes been put away?

Is my makeup organised in categories I can find what I need?

Is my hair brush free of hair?

General

Are the plants watered?

Are the bins emptied?

Bedroom

Is my bed made?

Is there fresh clean bedding for a bed change?

Bathroom

Is there enough toothpaste/floss/mouth freshener?

Are there enough toilet rolls?

Do I Deserve a Clean and Ordered Home?

I believe you deserve this in order to give you that inner sense of respect and luxury in your life. As a general rule of thumb, I organise my regimes into the following groups. Obviously the time needed will vary from household to household depending on house size and number of occupants.

I invite you to take a few minutes to use my template below and tailor to your personal needs.

Daily

Morning
1. Open windows to allow in fresh air
2. Start a clothes washing cycle (wash and dry)
3. Put dishwasher on/do washing up
4. Make bed
5. Clean kitchen/bathroom sinks/toilets

Evening
1. Tidy used items e.g. washing up/toys/makeup

Weekly

1. De-cobweb
2. Readiness score prep
3. Clean bathrooms

4. Clean appliances including inside fridge
5. Dust furniture
6. Clean mirrors
7. Vacuum floors/mop/steam floors
8. Change bedding
9. Empty bins
10. Ironing

Monthly

1. Clean inside kitchen cabinets and drawers
2. Scrub backsplash/grouting
3. Clean vents
4. Vacuum, damp wipe skirting boards
5. Clean doors
6. Wipe inside window frames and skirting board
7. Clean inside windows
8. Disinfect inside bins
9. Wash mattress and pillow protectors
10. Vacuum mattresses

Seasonal (the invisible jobs that transforms your health)

1. Clean out pantry/food storage areas. Remove out-of-date food
2. Wash or steam curtains and blinds
3. Clean inside closets and wardrobe changes

4. Clean freezer
5. Wash or dry clean duvets, pillows and throws
6. Clean carpets
7. Wipe down walls, ceilings and vents
8. Remove all furniture and clean behind/under

When To Tidy and When To Clean

I think we have all experienced not having enough time to do this. Other things easily become more important. Get rid of seeds of doubt in getting things done. The longer you neglect tasks, the longer the negativity lingers in your mind and even affects the quality of your sleep or the mood you wake up with in the morning. Self-discipline in cleaning and tidying builds sense of inner and self-confidence.

I always advocate cleaning in the morning. In Buddhist temples there is no such thing as cleaning after sundown. The daily routine of a Buddhist monk is to wash and dress then begin cleaning. They believe the fresh morning air fills you with energy and the silence helps you clear your mind for the day.

I am sure I must have been a Buddhist monk in a past life! I remember at fifteen years old, at my first job, I would arrive early to the call centre I was working at and vacuumed all the top floor before staff arrived. I don't think anyone knew I did it but it helped me mentally prepare for the day and by the time everyone arrived

I was ready and enlivened for the day. Little did I know at that young age that cleaning would become my career and give me the meaning I needed to be able to live a good life.

Tidying, on the other hand, is another matter and is best done before going to bed. A Buddhist monk knows how to tidy as they use things, but in a modern-day family home it's not always so feasible.

It's a good idea for your peace of mind and to help you feel refreshed in the morning to make sure everything is in its right place before bedtime and your spaces are ready for cleaning the next morning.

As I mentioned earlier, you don't need to spend much time cleaning each day but consistency is key. If you make an effort once a morning, even ten minutes will do and it will have such a positive effect on your mindset and spirit in how you approach the rest of your day.

I feel this poem by Raymond Isaacs helps encompass what we have been looking at:

Take one step at a time
and don't settle for anything less.
Use the power of your mind
to your full advantage to reach success.

Search deep inside to find
the inner you that brings out the best
achiever, victor and conqueror there is.
He, who will reach success by only climbing the stairs.

Take one step at a time
And not the easy way out.
In the path of life
You will have to overcome your doubt.

Failures you will have to face,
But that is what life is about.
And whenever an opportunity presents itself
Remember it's just one chance so you should go all-out.

Take one step at a time
Don't be hasty to get things done.
Remember to live your life right
Because you only have one.
And whenever you are trapped in darkness
Just look up and you'll see the sun.
And by just taking one step towards your future
Know that the battle you fight is already won…

CHAPTER FOUR

Zooming In

As soon as you honour the present moment, all unhappiness and struggle dissolve, and life begins to flow with joy and ease. When you act out the present-moment awareness whatever you do becomes imbued with a sense of quality, care, and love—even the most simple action.

ELKHART TOLLE

How Did I Discover "Zooming In"?

As part of my housekeeping journey I discovered something very magical. In order to be good at professional cleaning I noticed that physically I would zoom in to what I was cleaning right in front of my eyes. And it brought me right into the here and now, immediately.

I liken it to watching a movie and getting so immersed into what you are watching it's over so quickly you wonder where the two hours have gone? People often say to me, "I dread the cleaning part of life but when I actually do it, it feels therapeutic. Why is that?" I explain it's because your attention is outside of yourself for that time spent through zooming in with your eyes. You are having a break from that noise in your mind. The constant chatter of, "I hope I am not late for picking up the kids, I must ensure that I renew my insurance, I need new socks…" The list goes on. It's not always easy to do but I find it helpful when cleaning to try to consciously zoom in every few seconds or so. The more you do it, the easier it gets and the more nourishing the experience of cleaning becomes.

It became a "thing" in my business as an important part of my staff training programme. It's so easy when focusing on getting to your destination to forget to actually look precisely at what is right in front of us.

I wanted to reduce the complaints from clients saying, "The clean was great but some of the details were missing." After drilling into the complaints, I discovered that my team were actually doing the damp, dry, buff motions as discussed in Chapter One but were missing cleaning the details. Be it a cobweb, stubborn water or maybe a hard water stain.

We used to (back when I first started professionally cleaning) get complaints that we had missed things. It would be so frustrating as we knew we had gone through the motion and "covered the area" in question. We knew we had done the damp, dry, buff technique on the areas of complaint.

So I researched why. By addressing this zooming in technique we completely irradiated these complaints and we went from strength to strength and we started getting referrals to clean our clients' friends' homes too. We became indomitable as a cleaning company. I believe partly due to this principle.

Before this realisation I remember getting so frustrated, not understanding why we were getting these complaints. Once I discovered it was the finer detail needing extra elbow power, it came to me. I realised when I was looking at the detail I was physically zooming in with my eyes. I also realised, even though how obvious it appeared, most of us in our busy lives rarely consciously zoom in to the present fully into the here and now—what is right in front of us.

So I made myself practise zooming in at least once every seven seconds to get myself into the habit of it. It's that magic number seven again!

Most of us most of the time are focusing on other things in our mind. Like what will I cook for dinner? How is my son's work going? Did I remember to wash that T-shirt I need tomorrow?

I liken "zooming in" to a magical nature walk where I notice the beautiful details of a bluebell. The flicks at the bottom of the bell that look like a flick on a seventies hair style and the stripes on the bell that make them shimmer in the light. As opposed to driving by in the car where everything is seen from a distance and we miss out on the beauty of the detail.

Zooming in has two benefits:

1. It helped me to identify surfaces that need more than the quick damp, dry, buff technique (some extra elbow grease and scrubbing).
2. It brought me into the here and now and by doing so bringing me into a state of the present, resulting in inner peace. The normal outside chatter in my head just dissipated.

On my housekeeping journey I have been fascinated by the fact I started to heal as a woman. I have had a challenging life to say the least and many things happened that could have damaged me forever. The bad experiences used to haunt me daily and dictated my actions and I was on a negative wheel of self-fulfilling prophecies.

I truly put my healing down to this practice. Do you think you can benefit from practising this zooming in technique when cleaning? Or in fact in any job. If you are in a Zoom session at work, actually consciously look at the person talking. I liken it to sucking the attention out of your inner thoughts to what is happening right in front of you. You then notice the facial expressions, the colour changes in their skin—it allows you to notice more and maybe even help you engage and ask more pertinent questions to help you in your workplace.

My decision to be a housekeeper saved me in more ways than one. I realised that as I was cleaning I became so focused on what I was cleaning with the intention of making it perfect that the sense of time disappeared. The noise in my mind would stop. And little by little my inner wounds healed and I started to feel more at peace more of the time, rather than the other way round.

So cleaning does not need to be a chore or a thing to do just because we have to—it can actually be a healer and feed your soul inside out.

And when the end of the day would come and I would step back to look at my work, all I could do was smile. What job facilitates such a happy smile? Don't get me wrong, being a good housekeeper is demanding work but incredibly satisfying.

I have come across cleaners who, when pushed, said they only did it because they did not know what else to do and had to do it to get money to survive. They described how they just could not wait to get home to put up their feet and watch the latest TV soap. Their days dragged out and they resented the cards that life had dealt them. But it doesn't have to be this way.

Cleaning has been described as a low skilled job but truly I believe it's anything but that.

I don't know what brought you to read this book or where you are in your life but this I know. I can always look at things fresh and always start anew. All that is required is to be committed to the moment. When learning to dive you can stand on the edge of the boat for as long as you want, but in the end you just have to do it.

Cleaning to me is an act of pure love but first of all you need to love yourself. Dive overboard and give it a go.

Respect yourself by getting up and choosing to be present. Just doing it. Be it for your client if you are a professional, or perhaps for your family or friends or even if it's simply your own home. But most importantly for yourself.

Self-Value

I remember my mother saying to me I was special. I struggled with that for a long time as I grew up and tried to figure out why I was "special". Was it because I was better than everyone else? I wondered why that might be the case. Or was it because a god up there said I was privileged? Or was she just pointing out the obvious that everyone is special? I would then think that God was not fair giving me an advantage, I grappled with who I was and why I existed.

It took until I became a cleaner to learn to love myself from within and I believe this saved me. This is so simple but it's true. Through loving myself I began to believe and trust myself. I was the only one who could love myself. You can't make people love you. But the ironic thing I discovered was, when I actively showed myself the love and respect, it allowed other to do the same.

So at long last I feel special and cherish myself for who I am. Little did I know it would take me fifty plus years to get to this peace of mind and actually understand what my mother meant. Are there any areas of your life where you can actively show more love and respect to yourself?

When I first started cleaning I believed I was not good enough. I would clean really hard all day on impossible tasks and then have to offer the client free time to get it finished. I felt that I was not a good achiever and beat myself up for not finishing the whole house. I doubted myself. I remember looking down in shame that I was just not fast enough. I was always letting my client down in my own mind.

However, after much practice and by loving myself and applying myself to the tasks in hand, I began to believe in myself and value the work I put in on behalf of my clients.

Eventually, over time, I was proudly letting my client know that I had transformed their kitchen and if they continued to hire me I would get their whole house up to speed within a couple of months. My clients were more than happy to pay for this service. They then in turn experienced self-respect and love for themselves. The positive effects of cleaning are infectious.

I soon became known for helping to transform my clients' homes. And guess what? The love I gave to myself reflected in my work and in turn made my clients feel loved and supported. Then they in turn started to love themselves more through having pride in their own space. In turn that affected their family and loved ones too. Love flowing is truly infectious!

As a young woman I found myself in the business of change management. I mostly felt like I was a "fake" and didn't really know what I was talking about. I dreaded going to work. Little did I know that I would find myself through cleaning.

Until I mastered this zooming in technique through cleaning. Ironically now I feel like I am an effective change manager within my own successful cleaning business. I facilitate my staff to love themselves and follow this journey. I have come full circle thanks to the cleaning processes.

It's never too early or too late to find yourself. I am now in my mid-fifties and feel like I have a spring in my step and have a sense of wellbeing and purpose.

Benefits of "Zooming In" with Your Eyes

The eyes are the mirror of the soul and reflect everything that seems to be hidden; and like a mirror, they also reflect the person looking into them.

PAULA COELHO

Through zooming in to what's in front of you in a cleaning project it brings you into the here and now. The truth is to love yourself with the same intention you would if you were hanging on for dear life. All it takes is to commit to this. This is simple and true and in truth lies power and intention.

Come into the Here and Now

One of the biggest benefits of "zooming in" is that it brings you into the here and now and allows for full engagement in the task. When we are not fully present our mind is often somewhere else, which in turn results in being somewhere else and areas of cleaning get missed.

I often wondered why, if you follow the chunk-by-chunk process, how do things still get missed? Have you ever gone on a long drive, and your mind wanders and you have no idea for a few seconds where you actually are?

When my mother suggested I count sheep jumping a fence to get to sleep I remember trying desperately to stop my mind wandering—I could only get to the fourth sheep before my mind got bored and wandered away. How distracted do we get by outside noise and chatter?

The difference with cleaning is it's a physical job and requires intention so it's the perfect training ground to learn to be here and now and in turn connect with who you are and your own inner perfection and beauty. You are truly this love in essence. Practise this in your own home and it will ripple into other parts of your life.

Be Transported into the Present

"Zooming in" and being present helps us to appreciate the present moment more fully and we become more able to engage and even enjoy the present moment. This in turn leads to greater feelings of satisfaction and happiness.

As I am actively cleaning I am looking at the beautiful transformations I am making, right in front of my eyes. Through doing something positive it automatically attracts more positivity to you and in turn more joy in being in the moment.

This is why cleaning has helped me become happier with who I am and the choices I make. My mental health has skyrocketed as a result. People say cleaning is a mundane unskilled job that is only for the low end of society. I truly believe this to be a hundred percent untrue.

Maybe there is more truth than meets the eye to the saying 'positivity creates positivity'. To the contrary have you ever felt on a the opposite on a downward spiral. This practice can help change the direction from negative to positive.

Focus

Be fully focused on the task at hand... With practice this will become more and more natural. This in turn helps reduce stress and anxiety. Do you ever feel overwhelmed by your thoughts and worries about the future or regrets about the past?

Through consciously loving yourself, you will know that you have always done, and will always do, your best. If it's related to where you were or where you dream to be then as you work on the task in front of you (be it cleaning the inside of the toothbrush holder, cleaning the drain in your shower or vacuuming your floor) you will be transmitted into love—into the here and now. It will dissolve any stress and anxieties you may be having.

The more you do this, the more accustomed you become to doing it and the power of being present will naturally seep into other areas of your life.

I think if we taught housekeeping in schools many of the mental health issues now being faced by our younger generation could disappear.

Deep Breath

Something that helps me when I get caught up in my own thoughts and worries is to take a physical deep breath. And repeat this as many times as is needed until it helps me focus on the physical things and tasks in front of me. It helps bring ourselves into the here and now through focusing what's in from of us. Likewise in life in general and through focussing on clear objectives with mini tasks (like deep breaths) you will create a sense of satisfaction and motivation as you go along your daily journeys.

I remember as a child being taught transcendental meditation and breathing was an important part of the teachings in yoga and many other physical teachings. It really does work.

To illustrate a point, I have been diagnosed as bipolar. Less so now as a result of this zooming in technique I have followed over the years being a cleaner. I used to suffer extremes of negativity and then high levels of superficial positivity.

I would wake up in dread as to what drama the next day would unfold. I hated myself and beat myself up for attracting such adversity and negativity in my life.

Gradually through this practice I can truly say I wake up in the morning thinking about what wonderful things will come to me today and how I can bring happiness to those around me. Most importantly the feeling of dread is less and less.

It took time but this zooming in technique taught me how to be present and love myself as we are all uniquely made of pure perfection love.

I have yet to meet anyone who is happy all of the time and it's in this spirit I wrote this book. The more we do things that work, the happier we are more of the time, to the extent that you believe you will be fulfilled more than you are not fulfilled. The more we attain this level of being lighter, the more we embrace a breath to embrace the positivity.

As I transform people's homes and as my teams transform people's home and the more we all transform our homes, the more fulfilled we are. It's like a bank account: the more we put in, the more credit we have. Or the more exercise I do, the more it contributes to maintaining a healthy lifestyle. But it takes a little bit of work and a little bit of application but it pays off well.

The House as a Metaphor

By using the house as a metaphor for other parts of my life I have collated eight methods or techniques for you to use to try out when "zooming in". They are techniques that you may or may not be familiar with that can be used when you are faced with seemingly mundane tasks or a sense of lack of purpose or direction.

1. **Mindfulness Meditation:** Mindfulness meditation is a practice that helps to bring your attention to the present moment. It can be practised while focusing your attention on your breath and in turn the sensations in your body. Cleaning is quite a physical job and breathing helps you keep up the pace needed to do a good job.

2. Pomodoro: This involves breaking your work into short, focused intervals, usually twenty-five minutes in length separated by short breaks. This helps me stay focused on the task at hand and avoid getting distracted by other things. I have recently decided to take up running again. I am in my mid-fifties and was nervous to start as it felt overwhelming. On my first morning run I felt heavy and sluggish and nearly stopped after the first 100 metres thinking I could not do it. So I broke it down into twenty steps running then ten steps walking. I started with one mile, built up to two miles and then five miles. After that I tried to run a mile and it was a piece of cake. There is no way I could have done that on the first day back to exercise. So it's breaking down tasks into bite-sized chunks, then stepping and admiring the work like a clean toilet and sink. Before you know it, you will have cleaned a whole house, or run your first marathon.

3. Sensory Awareness: This technique involves paying attention to your senses by zooming in your attention to the look, the sounds, smells and feelings while doing a task. While I am rinsing the inside shower door with the hose, I listen to the sounds of the water shooting out of the shower and see the scum and soap disappearing off the glass.

4. Affirmations: Repeat affirmations like, "I am fully present and engaged in rinsing the dirty marks off this kitchen top." This is not for me but I do have a lovely cleaning lady on my team who you can hear talking to herself all day: "I am going to get this kitchen sink spotless" or "I am going to get these stairs pristine—you are not going to beat me"!

5. Acceptance: When you are resisting doing something while cleaning and you see that filthy toilet, you are probably thinking you would far rather do something else. I use the analogy of driving somewhere and you know it's a long journey in front of you. Your instinct is to try to speed up and your sense of urgency increases your stress levels. We have all witnessed that driver that drives up close behind you to speed you up. It does not get them there any quicker. In fact it just adds to a sense of anxiety.

They are constantly putting on the accelerator and then breaking and getting stressed with you that you are not going fast enough, even though you are slowing down due to the red lights in front of you. That feeling is that you are never where you want to be and that everything takes too long.

Everything around you becomes a problem. The weather, the road surfaces, the slow driver in front of you, the red lights, the boss that does not understand you. The list goes on. The sense of urgency and desire to be somewhere else can lead to feelings of stress and frustration. To be a good cleaner we have to master and accept being in the here and now. If things are rushed and we try to get away with doing as little as possible, it leads to a sense of dissatisfaction and the job not being done properly.

This is one of the main reasons I have to let a member of staff go when they really don't want to accept that to clean we need to focus on and accept whatever is in front of us. It takes courage to be a cleaner and I feel my courage and trust in myself has grown immensely through accepting the tasks at hand.

I used to criticise those clients for what I thought was living in an objectionable manner. Now I have learnt to accept what's in front of me and my clients notice the transformations but more importantly so do I. So the moral of the story is to do everything as it should be done and the process of a horrible journey disappears miraculously.

Ironically by doing things this way, you will automatically be where you are, in perfection and then paradoxically you will arrive quickly and effortlessly to the destination. The cream on the cake is a sense of accomplishment and satisfaction.

6. Forever Moment: One of my stranger techniques is to trick my mind, and imagine that where I am is forever. Now this is where you will probably start to believe I am nuts. My rational mind says that this is not true, of course, but I find the tension in my shoulders drops because the intelligent part of my mind recognises metaphysically this is where I really am all of the time.

All I have is the here and now and that is the gift of life. The other perfect example of the forever technique is when you are stuck in a situation where you are forced to wait, left to itself, my mind will be straining to go where I intend to be rather than where I am. I look at my watch constantly and listen to the announcements with frustration. But if I decide to sit there with the idea that this is where I am supposed to be, not where I am going, my experience changes dramatically. When I simply consider the idea that I am here where I am meant to be, I begin to look around at everyone else struggling with their impatience and realise I am in possession of a great secret: the secret of the forever people who were recently discovered in the Amazon rainforest.

7. This Is *Not* Forever: Conversely I look at the task in front of me and say to myself that this is not forever. This will end. I have a very remarkable and dear friend who had the most horrific childhood that involved terrible torture too awful to comprehend and that the only thing that allowed him to survive and pull through was the belief that this would *not* be forever—it would end. It helped put things into a different perspective. This builds great inner strength.

8. Building Personal Fitness: Last but not least, working on cleaning tasks, chunk by chunk, top to bottom, involves lots of physical activity. I have got a Fitbit and count the number of steps, achieving a minimum of 10,000 steps a day but sometimes a lot more and exceeding 20,000 steps a day. This gives me a sense of motivation to go for it. I have never felt stronger and healthier through attacking a good house clean with inner determination.

I often feel so lucky to have a job that keeps me fit and gives me endorphins that make me feel good!

Summary

By zooming into the present moment during something as simple as cleaning, you are engaging with life in a way that dissolves resistance. In that space, the challenges or negative emotions we carry seem to fade because our attention is fully absorbed in the task at hand. It's like stepping into a flow state where the mind becomes quiet, and the tension melts away, allowing you to simply *be*.

This approach not only transforms the task of cleaning but can become a metaphor for handling life's challenges. When we embrace the moment fully, rather than resisting or overthinking, the pain or struggle loses its grip on us. We align with life's natural rhythm, accepting that growth and learning often come through these moments of being present.

Do you find that this practice of melting into the moment during tasks helps you face larger challenges in life with more ease?

So to summarise, through "zooming in" with your eyes, cleaning tasks can be seen as a way to self-discipline and concentration, which are key aspects of many spiritual practices. By learning to approach seemingly mundane tasks with mindfulness and purpose, we are maybe able to find deeper meaning and fulfilment in our daily lives.

I so hope you enjoy practising this zooming in technique as much as I do and as a result have the most pristine home as enjoyable as those bluebells on a stunning spring woodland walk.

CHAPTER FIVE

Zooming Out

Pleasure is always derived from something outside you, whereas joy arises from within.

ECKHART TOLLE

Here is a beautiful discovery! By zooming in and focusing on the small, intricate details, you're not just cleaning but engaging in a practice of mindfulness. This level of attention pulls you fully into the present moment, where past worries or future anxieties have no place. In this state of flow, cleaning becomes almost meditative, where each movement is purposeful, and each task is approached with clarity.

It's fascinating how something as simple as cleaning can become a gateway to being more present, and in doing so, you can see both what needs attention externally (like dust or dirt) and internally (your thoughts and feelings). It's a very grounding practice. Do you find this state of mindfulness extends to other areas of your life as well?

Before looking into the art of "zooming out", there's a secret behind being a domestic goddess: it's showing up when you least feel like it.

We often mistake being a domestic goddess as someone who is immaculately dressed and has everything right under control, who magically makes running a home look easy. Being a domestic goddess is far more challenging but generates the highest rewards.

It's about showing up, stepping back (zooming out) and observing the consequences of our decision making and commitment to turning up. Not just when you feel inspired or when the conditions are perfect. Not just when you're in the mood—you turning up makes the difference.

Every. Single. Day.

This is the art of "showing up" —the hero and genius in any field.

It's easy to show up when you're motivated, when you've had a good night's sleep, when your favourite or best client is on the agenda. But what about when you're exhausted and maybe not well? When you're discouraged? When it feels like your work doesn't matter?

That's when showing up counts the most.

Because here's the truth: our feelings are fickle and actually don't signify anything. They change with the weather, with our blood sugar, with the last email or bill we received. If you wait to feel ready, you'll be waiting forever.

The domestic goddess knows this. They don't wait for inspiration to strike. They show up and get to work knowing full well that inspiration will follow.

Think about it. How many mediocre books have been published while brilliant ideas languish unwritten by "aspiring" writers waiting for the right feelings? How many businesses have failed to launch because the founder was waiting to feel "ready"?

Showing up isn't about perfection. It's about consistency. It's about building a body of work, day by day, regardless of how we feel.

But here's another secret: showing up changes how we feel. There's a magic in the act of beginning. Once you start, resistance fades. Momentum builds. What seemed impossible actually becomes doable.

This is why domestic goddesses never rely on motivation. They rely on intention. They create systems and plans that ensure they show up, regardless of their emotional state.]

The writer who writes five hundred words every morning before checking emails. The salesperson who makes ten calls before lunch, no matter what. The artist who spends two hours in the studio daily, preparing his tools and brushes to actually paint! They're not waiting to feel inspired. They're creating the conditions for inspiration to occur.

But let's be clear: showing up isn't easy. It's a practice. A discipline. More than that, it is a personal code. It requires overcoming the personal resistance that Churchill describes when confronting a blank canvass. He was timid until he saw a friend begin to "hurl slashes of blue on an absolutely cowering canvas. Anyone could see that it could not hit back".

It means pushing through the voices that say, "Not today", "You're not good enough", "What's the point?" or "It won't work anyway…"

It means showing up even when no one notices, when the results aren't immediate, when it feels like you're shouting into an empty space.

Because that's what we do. We turn up thereby making the difference.

We understand that success isn't about grand gestures or moments of brilliance. It's about the steady accumulation of small, consistent actions over time with conviction and enthusiasm.

We know that the ability to show up, day after day, is a superpower. It's what separates the amateurs from the pros, the dreamers from the doers. The show *must* go on!

So how do we cultivate this ability?

First, we need to redefine what it means to "show up". It's not about being perfect. It's about being present. It's about bringing yourself to the task at hand, whatever that looks like on any given day.

Second, we need to create systems that support showing up. By making this your personal code/plan you begin to develop an attitude that works.

Third, we need to practise self-compassion. Showing up doesn't mean pushing yourself to the brink of burnout. It means honouring your commitments while simultaneously honouring your real needs.

Fourth, we need to focus on the process, not just the outcome. Showing up is its own reward. The results will come, but we may not know exactly when. Trust in life's processes.

Fifth, we need to surround ourselves with others who value showing up. Work with people who also have these values. If they don't, invite them to learn.

But perhaps most importantly, we need to remember why we're showing up in the first place. What's your purpose and what is the work that only you can do?

What's the change you want to see in the home or around you? When we connect our daily actions to our larger purpose, showing up becomes not just a discipline, but has its own reward and contains the magic of positive consequences.

So the next time you don't feel like showing up, remember: your feelings are temporary and generally don't mean anything. Your personal code is what endures. However you feel, show up anyway. Do the work. Trust the process. In the end, being a domestic goddess isn't about how you feel. It's about you "turning up". This ultimately defines your legacy.

So, I discovered for me to grow and move forward in my life I had to show up. Making a difference is showing up.

Now, having said that, there is always a balance in life. As I grow older, now in my fifties, I push myself to continually run a little further and faster. But today I went out to run with the best good intentions but when I ran I felt aches and lethargic like I just did not have the energy. Wisdom is required to listen to my body and decide if I should "show up" despite these feelings or give myself a break and walk home.

Today I decided to walk home. I felt no shame as my body was telling me to rest. Learning when I should show up despite my barriers is a sign of wisdom—wisdom we all have within ourselves. We must learn to be kind to ourselves and know the difference between a barrier that can be overcome or a sign coming from your inner wisdom.

I believe your home should bring you a balance of outward pleasure as well as inward joy. A home should be a place pleasurable to look at but also inspire joy from within.

In this chapter we explore how, through "zooming out" with your eyes, you can train yourself to make your outer home beautiful and luxurious, but also a place where you feel safe, let your guard down and be yourself. Where you can find comfort and connection.

In this chapter we explore our environment which affects our mood, wellbeing and productivity. We have already discussed that unclogging is letting go of stuff we don't need or no longer serves us, which in doing so brings us joy.

Our behaviour is affected by our surroundings. You can use your spaces to help you to do things that bring you more happiness. We also all need a sense of safety and comfort and our home should help our shoulders relax and breathe calmly.

Living with order is better for the head than the visual noise of endless knickknacks shouting out for your attention. Keep them if they bring you joy or serve you somehow but otherwise let these things go.

Now in Chapter Five we go to the final stage of housekeeping. It's arriving to the top of the mountain. In fact it's called "finding home".

When I finish cleaning a room, any room, a kitchen, bathroom, bedroom, etc. I go to the door and I consciously zoom out with my eyes, look back at my work and allow the physical items in my room to flow in front of me with perspective, seeing my space as a whole. Take a few seconds to appreciate everything you have and how your space supports you. Gratitude is an essential part of enjoying your space—we often have so much more to be thankful for than we realise. As we discussed, everything in your home is made out of energy and the energy of each item transforms as you see the energy come from the relationship of "things" (physical items) to each other. I let their energy call out to me... be it positive or negative.

The "zooming out" technique allows us to see everything as a whole—it's a shift in perspective from the previous chapter "Zooming In". Do the following three things to bring harmony to your home. It's an important discipline to follow when completing cleaning a room. It's where your inner goddess gets to shine.

1. **Adjust** things slightly like a wonky picture frame. It corrects the energy of the room and sense of synergy.
2. **Move** things. Move your sofa to the left to receive the morning light for your morning coffee or move the main table to create more space around for the chairs and stop feeling so cramped. Again trust your gut instincts.
3. **Remove** things as in unclogging where things are not needed when you see them in relationship to all your things as a whole. Anything that stops you feeling the flow in your space, maybe it jars with you. Or does not bring joy or

detracts from the mood or purpose you want to create in the room. Items may need moving or simply removed.

How Did I Discover the "Zooming Out" Technique?

I have always been intrigued by the difference of what makes a cleaner exceptional as opposed to just okay. Through studying the cleaning practice myself with over 30,000 professional cleaning hours under my belt and by watching others clean, I came across a very exciting insight.

I realised that through the action of "zooming out" with my eyes at the end of each room clean, I could tweak, adjust and move things in the room to create a sense of beauty and luxury. In feng shui terms, "letting the energy flow".

It surprisingly takes much less than five percent of the time to clean a room but increases the sense of harmony and beauty one hundred percent, transforming a home from being just "nice and clean" to being "inviting, stunning and clean".

Through zooming out with your eyes it gives you a fresh perspective or what should be adjusted, moved or removed completely.

The Purpose of a Room

Before organising you home remember we want it to be a space where we can find connection and comfort. Imagine which activities you want to take place in your spaces that will positively impact your sense of wellbeing. Then it's about making it happen through shaping your living spaces.

Think about each room and the purpose of each room. For example, I want my bedroom to be a calming, soft and inviting room. So choosing soothing colours and shades that remind me of peaceful, positive thoughts and evoke happy memories is key.

Light

Embrace natural light where possible. Arrange your spaces to embrace the morning or evening light depending if it's where you have your morning coffee or enjoy an evening cocktail.

Lighting

I like to look at lighting too. Choose shades to suit the purpose of the room. In my bedroom I have soft lights with beautiful natural shades and patterns. Think about lighting as an artistic touch. Consider chandeliers, pendent lights and wall sconces that add glamour and sophistication.

Greenery

I love to incorporate nature and bring plants into my spaces alongside decor inspired by nature. Having certain greenery around your house can also improve the quality of the air too.

Activities

Create zones for different activities, where different things happen; this could include a space for painting, a cosy reading or meditation area, a lively musical area, a place to work, and a place to eat and sleep, play games or have drinks. Having clearly defined areas helps you keep things organised and tidy. Strategically placed furniture and furnishings support those happy experiences.

Sensory Pleasures

I love to incorporate sensory pleasures. I cherish the burning flicker of a candle, soft lighting, a gorgeous velvet fabric or the sound of uplifting music.

I remember when my boys were small I decided to introduce a lit candle to our evening meal. It had a wonderful impact on our experience. Rather than shovelling food down we began to slow down our eating and started to enjoy conversation as if being mesmerised by the flicker of the candle. Creating atmosphere can also be an important part to "finding home". Eating food transformed from a necessity to a time for recapping on the day's challenges and storytelling, making lovely memories as a family.

I periodically refresh and rearrange my home to keep it fresh and exciting just like when I first moved into the home. Small tweaks here and there can have a lovely impact.

Creating Atmosphere

Through zooming out with your eyes when assessing your space you can create an atmosphere which inspires you to feel motivated and engaged with your space.

Having a nice office actually helps me feel more creative and inspired. I have chosen some rich colours, with nice plants and some interesting art pieces.

Grouping

Through grouping my work folders and books into different sections and colour, when I look at them I feel organised and ready for whatever challenge faces me. I won't have to have my energy drained by spending half an hour trying to find a particular paper or book.

We have discussed that being organised and creating order helps reduce distractions and unnecessary, negative thoughts or frustration. This allows you to concentrate better and be less distracted. It actually supports your sense of accomplishment through discipline and the confidence it in turn brings to you.

Minimalistic Design

Add thoughtful and deliberate details. Embrace a minimalistic approach. Add clean lines with specially chosen accessories.

Infusing Rich Textures

Combine rich textures, like velvet, silk and linen, to add visual interest and a touch of luxury.

Natural Stone, Wood and Marble

If you are lucky enough to be able to choose your counter tops and flooring or accent walls, natural materials, like stone, wood or marble, can bring timeless luxury and elegance to your life.

Statement Furniture Pieces

Invest in well-crafted and elegant furniture that serves as a focus point in your space.

Why "Zooming Out"?

For the "zooming in" technique in the previous chapter I have been immersed in the detail of the clean.

In order to create order and peace in your home we need to step back to gain a perspective of the space in front of you. This is what I call "zooming out".

Only then can you notice if there are too many things on the mantelpiece, for example. Sometimes one vase and picture frame is more impactful than having flowers and five extra picture frames. Less can be more. You may notice a wonky picture, or the curtains are hanging unevenly. There is always a relationship between 'stuff' or 'things' in their physical form. Experiment with these dynamics for physical visual impact.

"Zooming out" with your eyes really does take less than five percent of the time it takes to clean the room. But it will help a room look its best. It's like when you put on an outfit and then you finish it off with those beautiful earrings, broach or scarf and it transforms the outfit completely.

You can do a brilliant clean and not do this five percent zooming out and the clean just won't have the wow factor we all love that can be achieved when we walk into an immaculate hotel room. This is what makes an exceptional domestic goddess.

Come from a Place of Love

If I am having issues with a room I close my eyes and take a deep breath and I pour love into the room! The purpose being to help me shift my emotion to a positive one. Then I look at it, "zooming out" with my eyes to see it from a different perspective. It helps me tweak things so the room pours love right back at me!

After cleaning each room, I "zoom out" with my eyes to look at the room as a whole. My relationship with the stuff and the space.

Through shifting my perspective to love, my inner natural instinct guides me when it comes to "zooming out". You do not need to be an interior designer to be good at it. Trust your own instincts and scan the room and stop at each point when you feel something is not quite right. Identify it. Rectify it. Play around with it. Explore different positions and places for your things.

It could be a cluster of "stuff" that needs sorting out. It could be the cushions looking disorganised, not plumped up or not colour coordinated. It could be the throws are hanging in a messy fashion. Maybe a plant is dying and needs water. Ornaments jumbled up. A rug may not be straight. Everything in a room should be presented back to you, throwing love back at you, and in return inviting you to engage with and be really comfortable in your space. Here we create positive alignment in our inner world and the outer world of "zooming out".

Trust Your Domestic Goddess

We all have a goddess within ourselves. Your inner goddess is how you feel about yourself when you hold yourself up to the light and trust in your love and inner beauty. Imagine the world looks at you the way in which you see yourself. And it begins with your own sense of self-worth. You are on a journey of creating your own unique signature visual brand that reflects your special and unique life experiences nd values.

However confident you feel about your homemaking skills, you have an innate ability to make things beautiful. It is something you are born with. You are unique and you will have a special *me* way of making a home beautiful and you can create your very own signature style depending on your values and your personality.

Remember, your unique view of the world is based on your experiences, values, your state of mind and the assumptions you have learnt to make on top of many, many other things that make you who you are.

I have trained hundreds of housekeepers and it has often struck me how Many start off having no confidence in their own homemaking skills. I get no end of pleasure in helping them find their own style and sense of outer beauty and style. I have learnt so much from watching people evolve with their own grace as they grow in confidence.

They say that by dressing well inside it can help you feel confident. It's the same with a home.

Your inner instinct for beauty is *definitely* inside of you. You can enjoy your own style. Like a shop creates a brand. I love The White Company and its products and looks. What is your unique brand? What brands are you attracted to? List them and note any similarities.

Since being on my housekeeping journey I have found my own signature style. I will share some examples.

I organise things into beautiful natural woven, rattan, seagrass or willow baskets to store everything in my home in groups from toilet rolls through to supplements, makeup, fruit, vegetables, etc. Basically anything that can be stored into groups. The baskets and storage holders are beautifully made and I love seeing their different shapes and natural beauty, rather than lots of individual items all over the place.

I love to have sheepskin rugs and beautiful neutral throws on certain chairs. I have lovely scatter cushions on sofas, chairs, bean bags and beds too.

I have unique smelling candles. Personally I love oud and spicy scents for an evening and fresh citrus essential oils around the home in the morning. I enjoy unusual and contrasting colours in closed spaces so they stand out in a natural way.

I enjoy having family pictures around the house put in frames to complement the colours of the furnishings. I update these every year.

I also have unusual plants with stunning shapes to complement the storage baskets, wall colours and furnishings. I make sure they are put in the best light to help them grow and be happy. There is nothing worse than a slow dying plant.

Finally, I have lots of large mirrors strategically placed throughout the house to create a sense of more space.

I would describe my style as luxury, cozy, shabby chic, which if I look back at my upbringing it's bringing together a bit of my mother's style, hippy shabby chic, and the more modern, luxurious style from my father. My style helps me relax and feel calm and happy.

You may already be sure and aware of your unique style and it can always be evolved, explored and updated as you grow and learn. You may discover something about yourself and your style through asking the following questions. Maybe you go on a holiday to a new country and take some of the experiences back to your home:

How would you I describe my personality?

What are my core values?

What are my strengths?

What colours represent my values?

What colours are luxurious to me?

What colours help me relax?

What shapes do I find attractive?

What type of landscapes inspire me?

Do I like greenery and what shades of colours?

What are my favourite plant shapes?

Do I like flowers? If so, what colours?

What are my favourite scents and why?

How do I like to store things in my home?

What home furniture brands to I like most and why? Minimal? Antique? Shabby chic? Modern? Cozy? Fun?

Who is my favourite artist and why are they unique?

Now describe my signature home brand:

The reason I am asking you to really think about your signature brand is that it reflects who you are. When you invite someone into your space, you are also sharing a bit of yourself and that will in turn directly affect the experiences you have.

If your purpose is to create a safe and warm space, you will be able to explore life deeper, learn more about yourself and make amazing memories. After all, is that not what a home is for? To help you have cherished experiences?

So the final process is to reflect on your life to date, to look back on it with the perspective you now have on life. Just like when you zoom out when checking your room for presentation and impact. This will in turn allow you to put everything into context and to choose what you want to give energy to in your life. It's like a computer reboot. After a while it has to be done to allow things to function at their optimum again. Give yourself a new lease of life. You deserve it.

What experiences can be let go of and what experiences can be cherished and remembered when you need them?

What are the top three things I am proud of about myself?

What are my top three accomplishments?

What are three things I would do differently in my past if I had the wisdom I now hold?

What have I learnt most about myself?

What does this say about who I am now?

How can my home reflect my inner wisdom further?

What three practical changes can I make to my living environment to demonstrate self-care and in turn nurture those around me in a safe beautiful place called "my home"?

1.
2.
3.

Breathing

As part of zooming out with my eyes I like to concentrate on my breathing as it brings me to the here and now and allows me to look at my surrounding from a crystal-clear perspective. Similar to when using the "zooming in" technique, the outside noise dissipates.

If you practise yoga or Pilates, you will be aware of these practices.

It goes without saying breathing is what keeps us alive. Whether we are awake or asleep we keep breathing, our blood flows, we digest our food and our heart beats automatically. But the one thing we can control is our breathing. When you are anxious your breathing is affected. By practising your breathing you can also help improve your state of being and your mind. To create a sense of balance.

Summary

"Zooming out" consciously, having finished cleaning a room, will allow you to give your home that extra deliberate "wow" factor that you truly deserve to have in your home.

To complete this book I want to share with you something I learnt to do that helped me in general in life, as a result of practising the zooming out principle while cleaning.

As part of my inner desire to learn and grow, through zooming out on my inner world (sounds like a contradiction but actually does work), I asked myself what causes the most stress in my home life? Three things came up for me immediately:

1. dirty oven
2. storage under my bed
3. high up lights and vents

Then I asked myself what areas cause me most stress in my business life?

1. legal compliances (what do I have to action and when)
2. training programmes for new starters
3. company accounts

Then I asked myself what causes me the most stress about my health?

1. being overweight
2. eating ready-made food
3. being dehydrated

Through taking a step back and zooming out on certain areas in my life that keep me the same, keep me blocked, I could see things more clearly. We get addicted to keeping the same problems as, although a frustration at least, they are frustrations we know hope to cope with and are familiar with. Our brain's function is to survive, even if it means staying the same. I found it fascinating when a therapist told me that as human beings we develop positive and negative patterns of behaviour. It takes conscious work to change old familiar patterns that no longer serve us. Through stepping back, like 'zooming out' we are able to decide with good perspective what patterns need to stay and which ones need to be replaced with new behaviours

If we look around at people in our lives, we notice particular friends and family who we love but have opinions such as they are overweight and will never change.

Real change takes time and discipline and we need to face the emotions linked to addressing a stress in our life. Facing my body being overweight made me feel sad and, dare I say it, depressed.

To change and grow I have to face the emotion when I get up early to run, which is apathy and upset. I just have to make mini steps to move through the emotions that these new behaviours trigger in me. I recently addressed the legal aspects of running the business. I worked out all the compliance dates required for all aspects of my businesses. I felt frustrated when working them all out. Now having come out the other side I have a spreadsheet with simple tasks I have to do each month. No longer am I stressed every morning that in the back of my mind I am missing legal deadlines. I now have space for something new in my life.

Be conscious that creating space for the new can, in the back of your mind, be more scary than facing issues head on. This is why the act of zooming out on your inner goals and personal stresses is a fabulous way of forming goals and mini steps along the way, leading to a more adventurous and enjoyable life.

So this is the perfect finishing touch! Zooming out after focusing on the details creates a holistic view of the space, allowing you to spot any small inconsistencies that can elevate the overall presentation. It's like stepping back from a completed painting to appreciate the full masterpiece and making those final adjustments that bring everything together.

This small step—taking a moment to adjust pillows, straighten items or align objects—can make the difference between a space feeling simply clean and one that feels truly inviting and visually stunning.

It's such a subtle but impactful shift, taking very little time but bringing immense satisfaction both visually and inwardly. The result is not only a home that feels fresh and calm but also one that reflects your mindful, intentional approach to life. Would you say that this balance between zooming in for details and zooming out for the bigger picture also applies to how you approach personal growth?

CHAPTER SIX

Conclusion

Through a myriad of experiences as a professional housekeeper and homemaker, I have discovered the keys to a happy and purposeful life. I hope you have enjoyed my story and find these principles both practical and symbolic, enabling you to embrace your unique brilliance and inner domestic goddess.

To conclude here are five affirmations for our cleaning principles:

Affirmation One: Cleaning with Water
"Through cleaning my home with the simplicity of water, I create a healthier, more harmonious environment for my wellbeing. I release the need for endless cleaning products and trust in the purity of water."

Affirmation Two: Unclogging Energy
"By releasing unneeded and unloved items, I open my home and my life to fresh opportunities and exciting new adventures. By

seeing physical items as energy—either positive or negative—I empower myself to be more intentional and ruthless in deciding what to keep and what to let go."

Affirmation Three: Chunk by Chunk (Step by Step)
"By following clear steps, chunk by chunk, from top to bottom, I care for my home and life with purpose. Steady and consistent progress ensures I am always moving in the right direction. Small setbacks are part of life's journey and can be embraced through trusting life's journey."

Affirmation Four: Zooming In
"By focusing on what's right in front of me, whether in cleaning or life, I embrace the challenges before me. In doing so, I become present, grounded, focused and at one with now, giving me a break from the unnecessary noise and chatter of the mind."

Affirmation Five: Zooming Out
"By zooming out and viewing my home with perspective and vision, I create a space filled with positive energy and dynamic flow. Through this broader perspective in life, I ensure I am shaping the journey I desire in life, crafting a home that reflects the experiences and joy I wish to cultivate."